Rachel,
for her, an inspiration!

*Enjoy the book
and
love your life!*

Just Imagine
Adventures with Teg & Esty

By
M. Faye Waters

水

M. Faye Waters

M. FAYE WATERS

JUST IMAGINE
ADVENTURES WITH TEG & ESTY

Published by:
Intermedia Publishing Group, Inc.
P.O. Box 2825
Peoria, Arizona 85382
www.intermediapub.com

ISBN 978-1-935529-14-9

Copyright © 2009 by M. Faye Waters
Printed in the United States of America

No part of this publication may be reproduced, stored in a retrieval system, or transmitted in any form or by any means – electronic, mechanical, digital photocopy, recording, or any other without the prior permission of the author.

All rights reserved solely by the author. The author guarantees all contents are original and do not infringe upon the legal rights of any other person or work. No part of this book may be reproduced in any form without the permission of the author. The views expressed in this book are not necessarily those of the publisher.

ACKNOWLEDGEMENTS

As a child, I would love to watch the clouds swirl in the sky as I daydreamed about my life to come. Once I became a parent, I wanted the same peace and possibility that I had imagined while engaging in this favored pastime.

Just Imagine came to me as I watched Joshua my son start to discover the world. Thank you Joshua... for inspiring me to create characters who can serve as great role models to the children of the world.

The first copyright was in the early 90's. However, as a busy parent, I placed the book on hold. Time flew by and what seemed liked minutes had turn into years. By the time, I picked up the book to write again, my son had moved away from home to attend college and I had just celebrated 20 years in the Human Resources profession. This only goes to show that you should never give up on your dreams.

Thank you to my husband Vern for allowing me the space to finally, complete the book. You are my soul mate and best friend.

Thank you to my parents for serving as great role models and for showing us what 54 years of wedded bliss looks like. You are a great inspiration to our entire family.

Thank you to my sister, Linda and her three daughters Chelsey, Taylor and Hannah for providing me great feedback. Get ready for the next book – it is in my imagination already.

A dear friend, Jodee Bock, provided her excellent editing skills early in the project. Thank-you Jodee, you really do rock!

Thank you Hans Gilsdorf – for taking my vision of these

characters and artistically bringing them to life in a very beautiful way!

Thank-you to the wonderful people at *Landmark Education* and *The Vanto Group*. From their distinctions, insights and wisdom I gained clarity and commitment to create and communicate the role models in *Just Imagine*. By truly understanding the virtues of integrity and honesty, our children and future leaders will live powerful and enriched lives.

A final and important acknowledgement goes to Alan Harrison. I am thankful and grateful for your clarifying edits, creative ideas, wisdom and guidance. Without you, *Just Imagine* would still be one of the best-kept secrets. I am thrilled to be on same path as we explore the world and its infinite possibilities.

As you embark on the journey of *Just Imagine*, I invite you to daydream about the people, places and things that delight and excite you. For me it is the thrill of seeing the faces of children light up as they read *Just Imagine*. Being part of something that allows them to live a better and more fulfilled life, is and will be one of my most cherished rewards in life. It is also seeing so many great children's causes created in the minds of those who are truly committed to making a difference in the world. A few of my favorites include Childhelp, RIF (Reading is Fundamental), the Boys and Girls Clubs of America and HUB (Humanity Unites Brilliance). Thank you to those organizations and the many others not mentioned. Together – we can and we will transform the world.

★ Throughout the book you will notice a star on the upper outside corner of a page. Star pages contain topics that provide great opportunities to engage in a dialogue with your friends and family. The stars are summarized as POINTS TO PONDER at the end of the story.

www.MFayeWaters.com

Contents

Chapter 1: Only a Few Clouds in the Sky	1
Chapter 2: Off to Town We Go	5
Chapter 3: Gone Fishing	13
Chapter 4: Sunday Fun with the Flicks	21
Chapter 5: The First Day of School	33
Chapter 6: Sweet Dreams?	39
Chapter 7: Up Above the Clouds	41
Chapter 8: The Calm after the Storm	47
Chapter 9: Someone to Watch over Me	55
Chapter 10: Back to the Search	59
Chapter 11: A Skeleton in the Closet	61
Chapter 12: Time to Go to Work	63
Chapter 13: Knock Knock	69
Chapter 14: The Search Continues	73
Chapter 15: Lesson of the Day	77
Chapter 16: All by Myself	81
Chapter 17: Now What?	85
Chapter 18: Another Missing Person?	87
Chapter 19: La La Land	91
Chapter 20: Out of the Dark	95
Chapter 21: Almost Time to Go Home	99
Chapter 22: Making it Right	103
Chapter 23: I'm Home	109
Chapter 24: The Future is Bright	113
Chapter 25: A Great Day for a Celebration	119

Chapter 1
Only a Few Clouds in the Sky

Val Flick, an eleven-year-old girl with a firecracker personality, lay on the grass daydreaming. The late summer sun warmed her as she watched the clouds go by. One of her favorite things to do was to imagine herself lying in the fluffy clouds looking down at all the hustle and bustle of the world below. Today as she peered up at the clouds, she spoke to them.

"Do you know that you look just like puffy people? I know you're not evil or scary, you're just puffy, happy people."

The bright white clouds swirled and moved into various formations as if her talking actually excited them.

"So what do you see in the clouds today?" asked a lanky fourteen-year-old boy walking toward the outstretched girl. Reese Flick plopped down beside his younger sister and looked up into the sky. Lightly taunting her, he pointed towards the sky. "Look, I think I see a monster — oh no and it's coming this way, it's — it's — it's a monster marshmallow!"

Val sat up and squealed. "Reese, stop teasing me!" Calming down, she continued, "I know that people live up there." She turned onto her tummy with her hands supporting her chin and gazed back at the clouds. "I just know it because I can feel it. Sometimes, I think they are watching me and that they are even waving at me. Besides, my dear bro, haven't you heard that it's good for you to take time each day to just be still and to take in the sights and sounds around you? Plus it gives a person a chance to be at peace with the world and themselves."

"Don't go all emo on me – but I suppose you're right," Reese said. "I wouldn't be your big brother if I can't find something to bug you about."

Flashing him a crooked smirk, she looked beyond him to a large cloudbank. Val thought for moment. "It would be so fun jumping from cloud to cloud and looking down at all the people, and all the different places in the world. jiit-Now! Living up in the clouds would be uber cool."

"What is that you said?" asked Reese.

"I said it would be cool to live in the clouds."

"No. What was the word you said first?"

"Oh – you mean jiiT-Now. It's a word that I made up that stands for 'just imagine it now.'" jiiT-Now inspires me and helps me think that anything is possible. jiiT-Now allows me to forget some of the petty things in life and helps me choose to see the good in everything and everybody."

"Doesn't it sound like a swear word that mom and dad told us not to say?"

"Maybe, but they won't care when they realize what I'm really saying." Getting back to her cloud gazing, she sat up. "I know what I'm going to do!"

"What now?" asked Reese.

"I'm going to name some of the clouds," Val said emphatically.

"Val! Reese! It's time to drive into town!" A voice in the distance interrupted them just as Val was thinking of names for the puffy people. The two kids jumped to their feet, brushed the grass off their clothes and started walking down the hill toward the family car.

Val looked up into the sky whispering, "Goodbye cloud people, I'll see you later!" She looked down the hill toward the car, and as she glanced back up into the sky, she saw a sparkle. She could have sworn that one of those puffy people had just winked at her.

M. FAYE WATERS

Chapter 2
Off to Town We Go

As Val climbed into the back seat, her mother greeted her in a firm, yet gentle voice. "Val you didn't sweep the floor last night and I expect that when we get home you'll do it right away. It's all a part of helping out in this family."

Jean Flick a small, frail woman is regarded by the community as "the woman with a heart as big as the sky." Of her many talents, what she loves best in life is being a wife, a mother and a friend.

On this Friday, Jean and her husband Al are taking the kids to town. "I don't know what I would have done if we hadn't taken the day off," she said to Al. "It's a good thing that Fridays are usually slower in the summer. We really need to get organized and catch up on things before school starts on Monday."

Looking into the rear-view mirror Al spoke to Val, "It also helps when we get the chores done so we have time to go school shopping."

The family farm was only four miles from town and to Val it

seemed like the ride was taking forever.

"Here it comes — Tickle Tummy Hill!" Al, a distinguished looking man, loved to joke and have fun with his children. "We're almost there!" He started to speed up the car and just at the very moment they reached the top of the hill, he took his foot off the gas, causing everyone's stomach to flip flop.

They were all giggling hysterically as they continued the trip into town. Even though Val and Reese felt they were getting too old for their dad's jokes and horseplay, they went along with it anyway.

Val and Reese needed to pick up the last of their school supplies at the General Store. Val was especially looking forward to seeing the storeowner Betty. As they drove over the last hill, a small town came into sight. Perched on the banks of the James River, sits the town called Manfred.

The small town boasted of one church, the ancient Grand Hotel and next to the hotel, Stella's Cafe. At the south entrance was a gas station, two seed and grain elevators, and the post office where Val's father worked. After he closed up each day, he would head home, eat with the family and go out into the fields to farm the land that his grandfather and great-grandfather had once tended. A two-story brick schoolhouse stood at the north end of town. The majestic building had stood with grandeur for more than fifty years. It featured some of the finest wood moldings in the state and had a bell that was hand-hammered in 1959.

Al stopped the car in front of the General Store and the family piled out and made their way inside. Val quickly glanced around the store looking for Betty. Turning the corner by the candy aisle, she ran smack dab into another girl whose wild eyes and hair were black as the darkest night. As they looked each other up and down, Val felt a queasy feeling starting to churn in the pit of her stomach.

"Here — have a piece of candy!" The dark-eyed girl thrust a jawbreaker toward Val.

Val reluctantly put out her hand and accepted it.

The stranger continued. "My name is Tempest, and my Dad owns the big grain elevator. You know the place where all of the farmers buy seeds from us and sell us their crops. Anyways, we just moved into the Nicholson mansion!"

"I, ah, I'm Val. Thanks for the candy."

"Well, next time you will owe me. But don't worry - you can pay me back later," proclaimed Tempest as she quickly darted off.

Puzzled by the exchange, Val continued on her way to Betty. As soon as they made eye contact, Val forgot about Tempest and the bewildered look on her face immediately turned into a big smile. The two reached each other with open arms and hugged as if they had not seen each other in a very long time.

Betty, a woman in her early sixties, had spent her entire life running the General Store. Her mother had died of cancer when she was only three, so she grew up alone with her father. They lived above the General Store, making it easier to run the business. Her daily routine had always consisted of helping her father stock shelves and wait on the customers. When Betty was in her late twenties, she had the choice to marry several men, but none would allow her to keep running the store. Instead, she chose the family business over all of them. Her father passed away just last year right before his 100th birthday. Betty lived a lonely life now and looked forward to seeing Val's bright, dancing eyes. "Oh it's so nice to see you!" Betty exclaimed as she hugged Val. "I saved for you some pencils that I just know you will like for school. I'll go get them."

During the summer on the days, that Reese had other plans; Val would ride into town and stay while her parents worked. She filled her days by running small errands for the elderly people in Manfred. Her most favorite task is helping Betty to restock the shelves. Sometimes she would sit and watch Betty play solitaire and listen to her stories from the past. Betty's Uncle Roger and his family often watched the store while Betty and her father traveled to exotic locations. Those stories were so intriguing to Val that she could not wait to see the world herself.

"Here you go." Betty handed her the pencils.

"Thanks. How much do I owe you?" Val reached for her coin purse. "I've been saving up the money from the vegetables we've been selling."

Betty smiled. "They are a gift and I want you to enjoy them. Besides, it feels good to be able to give something to someone who gives so much to me."

"But what I have given to you?"

"You've given me the gift of friendship."

"Well thanks!" replied Val as she moved her attention back to the pencils. "Oh, I love this blue one with little clouds. Ever since you told me the story about you and your dad visiting the mountains in North Carolina, I keep dreaming of standing on top of the tallest one and looking down at the valleys and the people below. Sometimes I dream that I'm standing high up in the clouds and I can see the whole wide world."

Betty listened attentively as Val continued. "It's really neat standing in the clouds. The sun is so warm and I can see all kinds of people going to work or running their kids to all kinds of places. It's just so peaceful and so quiet."

Betty smiled. "Sounds like a pretty real dream to me."

Just then, Val's mom appeared at the counter. "It will be another ten minutes before we're ready to pay for our things. If you want, you can go play in the park until we're done.

"Okay, Mom." Val hugged Betty. "Thanks again for the pencils. See you in church on Sunday."

As soon as she stepped outside, Val heard, "Silly Sally, Silly Sally wears ugly clothes and sleeps in an alley!" Tempest was teasing Val's BFF. Val walked over to the girls, and not knowing how to react, she froze. She ended up standing by Tempest, which made it look as if she were going along with the teasing.

At that moment, Val's parents came out of the store. Her dad, unaware of what had just happened, said, "Come on Val, it's time to go."

Val turned to listen to her dad and as she turned back, Sally gave Val a heartbroken look, turned and ran off crying, humiliated. Tempest turned on her heels and strutted off toward the block where she lived.

Still not realizing what had just taken place, Al announced, "Since it's a family night out, let's stop at Stella's and have something to eat before heading home. I am buying. Besides — the cook deserves a night off."

He put his arm around Val as he waved good-bye to Sally and the dark-eyed girl, who had already run off. Shrugging his shoulders in confusion, he directed Val across the street and to the restaurant, joining Reese and her mom at the door.

With its quaint, historic charm, Stella's had some of the best food for miles around. The host seated them in a booth by the window. From where Val sat, she could see the park. She looked sadly out the window and watched her friend Sally crying. Once again, Val felt sick to her stomach. All she could think of was the hurt look on Sally's face.

The waiter appeared at the table. "Well, hello family Flick. It's nice to see you out this evening."

"Hello Mayme, it's nice to see you too," replied Jean.

"I'll take your order if you are ready?" The family ordered and Mayme went off to place their order and get their drinks.

Seeing that his daughter looked upset, Al decided to go on a joke-telling binge. "So why couldn't the animals play cards on Noah's Ark?" After a long silence, everyone looked to see if Val would respond.

Since she did not even care to offer a reply, Reese chimed in. "I don't know. Tell us why, Dad."

Al smiled, acting as if they should know the answer, declared, "Because Noah was standing on the deck."

They all laughed. Even Val chuckled slightly as her dad leaned over to give her a hug. He continued on, "Why can't a prince be twelve inches tall? Without waiting for anyone, he blurted out. If he was, he would be a ruler." Chuckling again, he said, "Okay, I can see this is a tough crowd, so I'll only tell one more. What happened to the man who stole ten bars of soap? He got away clean." The whole table laughed, knowing that it gave him pleasure to brighten their day with his light-hearted humor.

The food came and Val ate as she listened to her mom and dad talk about the family who just moved into the Nicholson mansion.

"Val's teacher, Mrs. Rogness said that the house was built in 1928 and is considered to be some of the most expensive property in this region," said her mom. "They must really have a lot of money to buy such a house."

"Yes," her dad replied. "However, money can't buy happiness. By simply being grateful and acknowledging what we have, we will attract true wealth and abundance. It's just one of those universal laws." They finished eating in silence, wrapped up in their own thoughts.

Getting restless, Al squirmed in the booth. "Well it's time that we head for home." He paid the bill and they all got up. "Good night Mayme, thank the cook for another great meal." After they all said good night to the staff, they walked out into the evening.

The drive home was silent as they watched the sun make its way down the horizon in a beautiful orange glow.

Once home, they put away the groceries, Val, and Reese excitedly put their school supplies into their backpacks.

"Not that we're still hungry, but who wants popcorn?" Al knew the family ritual, and everyone jumped up to join in.

"I'll get the butter out," said Val.

"I'll get the popcorn," continued Jean.

Al added his contribution. "I've got the kettle."

Plopping several bright colored plastic bowls on the counter Reese added, "Here are the bowls." They popped the corn and settled in to play a game of gin rummy. Soon the grandfather clock in the foyer chimed ten o'clock.

"Time for bed," said their mom. The kids got up and walked up the stairway to their rooms.

Helping Val to get a book off the top shelf of her bookcase Reese stated, "Remember, if dad does his thing again tonight, we need to have fun with it."

"I know, but sometimes he treats us like we're little kids."

"It's just his way of showing us that he loves us."

"FE FI FO FUM, I smell the blood of an Englishman!" Their father was coming up the stairs to hug them goodnight. He loved that line from *Jack in the Beanstalk*. Val's bedroom door was open, so he popped his head in the room. Again, he deeply bellowed, "FE FI FO FUM!" as he lurched towards them, he grabbed them both and started tickling them. They all fell to the floor laughing.

Jean walked into the room as they were all getting up off the floor. "It's time to say our prayers," she said.

Val jumped into her bed as her dad and Reese sat down beside her. In unison, they all said their nightly prayer. "Now I lay me down to sleep, I pray the Lord my soul to keep, if I should die before I wake, I pray the Lord my soul to take." Val hugged both of her parents as they tucked the blankets around her.

"We love you!" said her mom.

"I love you too!" replied Val. As the trio left the room, her Mom half teasing, said, "Good night and don't let the bed bugs bite."

Chapter 3
Gone Fishing

In the muffled darkness of the house, the grandfather clock bonged out seven bells. Only a faint light was coming from the grow light positioned by a large group of plants. The door to Val's bedroom opened as a shadow of a person made its way across the room toward her bed. A hand rose up and landed on her shoulder.

Reese shook Val awake. She jumped slightly as he whispered, "Shhh — get dressed and meet me out in the hallway."

She dressed in several layers and quietly opened her bedroom door. Their parents peeked out of their bedroom door and watched them as they crept down the stairway. Smiling at each other, Al and Jean knew this was going to be an adventure for both of them.

Val and Reese very quietly went into the kitchen and Reese started to make sandwiches. "Here, this is the way I like to make my sandwiches – just a little peanut butter on both sides and lots of jelly in the middle," he said. "But I don't cut it fancy like Mom does because the extra jelly that I put on would fall out."

"Let me do mine." Val used the squeeze container to form a star on her bread. "There, a star for a star!"

They packed their lunch into a backpack, which Reese threw over his shoulder. He opened the screen door of the kitchen and the pair slipped out into the foggy morning. "Today, I'm going to teach you how to fish!"

He started to speed up a little. "I remember when I was six. Grandpa would wake me up early. It seemed like there was no one else awake in the entire world – that is how early it was. He would make us waffles and we would eat them, pack up our stuff and then we would be off."

Reese proudly lifted an old leather tackle box in front of Val. "Grandpa Henry gave me this to take care of and said it's my job now to keep it straightened and full of lures and that kind of stuff."

The sun rose over the hill and reflected on the water. Reese and Val reached the old bridge and started to get their fishing poles ready. Reese dug up some worms out of the black ground and Val squirmed as he put a couple of worms on her hook. She squealed as one dropped on her foot. "Ugh — I'm not so sure about these worms."

"Val, you're not worried about a little old worm. Heck you're the one who is always picking up strange bugs and things."

"But this is different, you dug it out of the ground and it's full of slime and dirt. I pick up ladybugs and those kinds of things, and besides they're not slimy."

"Well some ladybugs bite, so be careful." Reese finished preparing her hook and handed it to her. "Now we're ready to catch the big one."

After nearly an hour, Reese felt a tug so hard that he thought he would have fallen into the water if it were not for the railing on the bridge.

"Whoa! Slow down fish so I can catch you!" He fought hard to hold on and kept reeling it in just as he learned how. Finally, he pulled out the biggest walleye he had ever seen.

"Oh boy, Mom and Dad will be so proud of us," Val exclaimed excitedly.

As Reese took his fish off the hook and attached it to the stringer, Val felt something pulling on her line "Reese. Hurry up. I think I've caught one too."

Reese helped her reel in the fish. "This is a great fish, Val," he said.

"Yeah, but it's not as big as yours."

"That doesn't matter," he said.

They fished a while longer and Val said, "I'm getting hot, can we go swimming now?"

"I guess so; it seems that all the fish are in school. Get it, school?!" Reese joked.

"No, I don't get it."

"Well, a group of fish swimming all together is called a 'school,'" he explained.

"I'm just kidding. Of course I know what a school of fish is ...I just wanted you to feel brainy."

"Now that it's the end of summer, the water will start to cool off, so we had better get one more swim in," he said. "Remember, we can only swim within the orange markers." As he pulled off the pants that covered his swimsuit, he shouted at Val. "Last one in is a rotten egg!" Reese waited for Val to catch up, and then they both started to run into the water at the same time. He faked tripping at the last minute and let Val believe that she won.

They swam and splashed with each other. Val got distracted playing with some of the willows then realized she was alone.

"Reese, where are you, I can't find you!" Val cried out nervously as she circled around in the water. "Reese, pleeeease, I want you to come out now, this isn't fun anymore."

"I'm right here." Laughing at her, Reese dove out from the trees where he had been hiding.

"I don't want to play anymore." Val pouted. "I didn't know where you were, and I was afraid something happened to you."

"Nothing is going to happen to me, so don't worry."

"Well, I'm getting tired and I want to warm up in the sun."

"I guess it's time for a break." Reese waded toward the shore. They crawled out of the water, laid out the blanket, and plopped down on it. Lying down and looking up at the sky, Reese said, "Wow, look at how fast the clouds are moving today."

"It looks like they're in a hurry to get somewhere," Val replied.

Reese pulled their sandwiches out of the cooler-pack and once they finished eating them, they each plopped on their backs and watched the sky in silence, each wrapped up in their own daydream. Soon Reese interrupted the silence. "I think it's time we pack up our things and walk back home. Mom and Dad said they'd make us an early supper if we brought some fish home … and these fish will be a great plenty."

They stood up to put their clothes on. Val pulled on her shirt and looked around. "Do you ever get a feeling that we're being watched?"

"Sometimes," Reese answered, "but it makes me feel good."

As they walked back home, they came up to an old, but cute, cottage. "Is it true that Mrs. Palmer is crazy?" Val had heard the rumor at school.

"No," replied Reese, "it's just that she lives with a lot of cats. That does not make her crazy. She's just keeping herself company."

As they got closer, Val and Reese saw that Mrs. Palmer was in the yard weeding her flowers. She noticed the pair and waved to them.

"Hello kids, have I got something for you. I'm just about to take a rhubarb dessert out of the oven and it's the best when it's hot and the ice cream melts over the top of it."

"But we have to get these fish in cold water or get them cleaned," said Reese.

"Nonsense, I'll put them in water here and I'll call your parents so they don't worry about you. I've been so lonely out here; it's nice to see some familiar faces. Come on in now."

Val and Reese handed the fish over to Mrs. Palmer and followed her into the quaint cottage. After she put the fish in water, Mrs. Palmer, true to her promise, removed the dessert from the oven, added two scoops of vanilla ice cream onto each plate, and set them in front of the kids who plopped down on chairs at the dining room table.

"Here you go."

The kids were not shy about digging into the delicious treat.

"It's so nice to have guests. I get so lonely out here. Most people around town think that I have lost my marbles. But I tell you what – my mind is as sharp as a tack." The pair kept eating and listened as she continued. "I really wish that people didn't make judgments about others without knowing all the facts. For that matter, we should not be judging each other at all. The world would certainly be a kinder world! As my oldest son, Randy would say, 'Judging should be reserved for contests and in his case, it would be car shows."

Just as the kids took their last bite, Mrs. Palmer plopped a big photo album on the table. "Here, let me show you some pictures of my family and of some of the fabulous cars that Randy restored. My younger son, Corey has also gotten into the same hobby. So I have lots of pictures of them, their cars and their trophies."

Before they knew it a clock chimed 4:00 p.m. "We really need to get going now," said Reese. "Thanks so much for the dessert."

Val rubbed her tummy saying, "Thank you. That was scrumptious."

Mrs. Palmer looked sad at the thought of her company leaving. "Well, be sure to stop in whenever you can. I suppose with school starting, it will be Halloween before I see you again."

Both waved goodbye and thanked her again, as they started their way back home.

Just as they got to the front door of their house, their dad walked out of the garage. "Welcome home, fishermen — or should I say fisher people. Here, let us look at those fish. I think these are worth taking a picture of," he said proudly.

"Well, I just happen to have a camera." Their mother appeared with the digital camera. "Okay, say cheese — or would that be leech."

"I'll fillet the fish, but only if you two watch, so you understand how to do it." Their dad was always ready to take advantage of a teaching moment.

"After supper, I think you two had better take a bath or a shower. You smell like a combination of fish and swamp," said Jean as she sniffed the air surrounding the pair.

Together the family made vegetables and the fish on the grill and ate their meal outdoors. They chatted about their fishing expedition and their visit with Mrs. Palmer. Unexpectedly, Val asked, "Dad, do you think people live in the clouds?"

"That's a good question. What makes you ask?"

"Oh — it's just a feeling that I have. It's like they watch me all of the time."

Val's parents exchanged looks, but listened intently. Val added, "They're not scary; it kind of makes me happy knowing that they are up in the sky, looking out for us."

"Well, I'm glad they are friendly," said Jean. "After all, your favorite pastime seems to be watching them and I'd hate to think that you found them frightening. It is starting to cool off and the sun is going down. It's time that we get this mess cleaned up and head back into the house." They carried everything into the kitchen.

"I'll help your mother with the dishes, and the two of you need to get cleaned up," said Al.

The fishing pair turned and went upstairs.

After the two had bathed, they came downstairs in their pajamas. "Now doesn't that feel better?" asked their mother. They nodded "yes" as she hugged them. "And you smell much better too. Your dad has a movie ready, and he just started a nice fire in the fireplace for us."

As Reese walked into the family room he asked, "What is the movie of the night Dad?"

"We're going to watch the video of our family reunion last summer." No sooner than he started the movie, he was already laughing. "Look at Uncle Paul dance. For a big guy, he sure is light on his feet."

Reese chuckled. "Yeah, and look at Cousin Andrew bouncing that basketball. The ball looks as big as he is."

The family laughed and continued watching the home movie.

Chapter 4
Sunday Fun with the Flicks

The next morning was Sunday and Val and Reese sat on the large porch swing watching a hummingbird at the feeder as they waited for their parents to get ready for church. Their mother loved hummingbirds and kept the feeder filled at all times. Reese broke the silence. "Did you know that hummingbirds can fly backwards and upside down, and that their wings beat about seventy times a second?"

Jean walked out onto the porch. "You'll learn all kinds of neat things like that, Val, when school starts again tomorrow." In a reminiscent voice, she added, "your Grandmother Gena used to say that hummingbirds and teenagers have a lot in common. They move faster and eat more often than the rest of us. They fight with each other and have trouble sharing but they are so beautiful to look at." The telephone rang and she went back into the house to answer it.

Jean listened intently to the caller. "Oh dear … is she okay?" She listened for a few seconds and continued. "I am so very sorry. I will talk with Val about this right away. I do not know what would possess her to do something like that. Thank you for calling. Again, I am so sorry. I will see you in a few minutes at the church. Goodbye."

"Val – Reese, it's time to leave for church!" she called out as she stepped out onto the porch.

Before Val could climb into the back seat of the car, her mother stopped her. "That was Sally's mother on the phone. I understand you were hanging out with Tempest Matador on Friday. She said that you were teasing Sally about her clothes. For heaven's sake Val, what has gotten into you?"

With her head to the ground Val mumbled, "I really wasn't hanging out with her, I had just walked out of the store when she was teasing Sally and I just stood there because I didn't know what to say."

"Haven't you ever heard of 'guilty by association'?"

Val shook her head. "No. Not really."

"Well, it's when it looks like you are participating or guilty, because you're with a person who is doing something wrong. Plus, when you don't do anything about it, people think that you are just as guilty as the person who is doing whatever it is." She took a deep breath and continued. "If that's the case, I think you need to explain what happened to Sally and apologize to her after church. The longer a person waits to apologize for any wrongdoing – the more hurt and damage there is. Now let us get going before we make ourselves late. I also expect that you won't be doodling and will pay attention once we get into church," she added in a firm, yet gentle voice.

Before walking around the car, she hugged Val. "You're a good girl with a kind heart and I'm not so sure about you hanging out with this girl Tempest, especially if she's going to tease other kids. This is just the beginning of our conversation. We need to talk about this when we have more time."

"Boy is that right, things are just beginning," Val thought to herself as a queasy feeling started again in the pit of her stomach.

Jean was worried about Val's new acquaintance. She had never known Val to tease anyone. She knew that at some point in her life that Val would come across such people. Nevertheless, she did not want to let go of the sweet little girl that she knew as her daughter — a young girl who, up until a week ago, thought kindly of everyone she met. The only worry Jean and Al had ever had about Val was what injured wildlife she would bring home to nurse back to health.

Al sensed heaviness in the air and tried to break the tension. "We're almost there — Tickle Tummy Hill!" The family car went over the hill. Today Val's tummy did not tickle as much as it felt nauseous from being on a wild ride at the county fair. Val was not sure if it was because she had disappointed her mother or because of Tempest Matador, the so-called friend she had just met on Friday.

Al brought the car to a stop in the church parking lot. Quietly, the family got out of the car and walked into the church. They nodded and smiled "hello" to their friends and neighbors as they made their way to their usual pew. Val felt her stomach jump and churn as she walked by the Matador family.

The first hymn started and Betty's heart swelled with pride as Val sang sweetly in the row behind her. After finishing the song, the congregation sat down to listen to the announcements. "We have a new family to introduce to our church and our community," said Pastor Johnson. "Craig and Esther Matador, along with their children

Tempest and Matt, have moved into the Nicholson house. Please, help them feel welcome."

After church, Pastor Johnson shook hands and greeted everyone as they left the church. As the Flick family approached him, he suggested, "Val, you and Tempest should get to know each other since you'll both be in the same grade at school and in Sunday school today."

Val responded in a heavy voice. "Yeah, we've already met." Off to the side she could see Tempest smirk and look away.

When church was over, it was the ritual for all the parents to go down to Stella's to visit over coffee while they waited for Sunday school to dismiss. As the parents parted, the children gathered into their groups. Once the classes were over, the children poured out of the church amidst loud chatter.

Reese took the lead. "It's time to walk to the park." The kids walked the few blocks downtown to join their families.

Val avoided Tempest at the church and during the walk to Stella's. She ran over to Sally and stammered, "Sally, we need to talk. I feel bad about what happened yesterday. I know it was wrong for me not to say anything or to stick up for you. It's — it's — it's just that I didn't know what to do. Tempest had just given me some candy and talked about…" Val, trying to mimic Tempest, sputtered, "how I would owe her." Val then continued softly. "Anyways, I'm so sorry, it was wrong and I hope you'll forgive me."

Sally finally looked up at her. "Oh, I'm so happy. I thought we would never be friends again. Tempest is so mean."

"I know." Val was quiet. It did not take long for the two pals to link arms as they skipped and danced the rest of the way. Many of the kids liked to stop at the General Store before joining their parents. They giggled and chattered while they made their way through the entry, greeting Betty as she waved them all in. They stopped to look at the Halloween display full of decorations and excitedly talked about everything they wanted to buy.

Sally perked up and whispered to Val. "Let's go to the park and swing!"

"Yeah, let's go."

They left the store and broke into a run to each grab a swing. Soon Val's parents came out of Stella's and waved for the kids to come and get ready to go home.

On the drive home, Val could hear her parents talking about the Matadors coming to Manfred to buy a seed and grain elevator and to start up a new gas station so they can "run the other one out of town." She heard her mom say, "It sounds like a lot of the folks are worried about Craig Matador's intentions." It was very unusual to hear this coming from a woman who never encouraged gossip.

Her dad looked off into the fields. "Unfortunately, the Matadors can afford to do whatever they want."

Val felt things had been changing ever since the Matadors arrived in town. She peered out the window and saw some the darkest clouds she had ever seen moving wildly in the sky. "The clouds even seem to be stirring up their own trouble, just like things in Manfred," she thought to herself.

Al pulled the family car into the garage and shut off the engine. They all got out of the car and walked quietly into the house. Each of them was deep in thought once again.

On Sundays, the Flick family traditionally shared in making lunch, so Jean broke the tension. "Today we're having Sloppy Joes."

"Don't forget the secret ingredient," added Reese. They all got busy in making the family meal, trying to forget about the trouble that seemed to be brewing. They all felt comfort in knowing that the secret ingredient was just a pinch of organic brown sugar.

"Guys, why don't you go and set the table outside for lunch? Val and I have a few things to talk about."

As soon as the door closed behind them, Jean empathically asked, "So tell me what happened with you, Sally, and Tempest?"

"Looking sadly out the window, Val replied, "It all happened so quickly and I just wish I could do it all over again. All I did was stand there – so of course Sally thought I was with Tempest. I did apologize to Sally and we're back to being best friends."

"In life there are very few do overs and the important thing is to learn from our mistakes. With age, more wisdom does come and I wish I could simply bestow onto you what I have learned the hard way. However, going through something like this makes you a better person. When people experience the low or bad part of something, it allows them to enjoy the high or good things in life even more. We simply become more grateful for what we have.

"Thanks mom, I'm so glad that I can talk to you about anything."

"I really hope that you will always feel that way. Unfortunately, it is common for children and teenagers to think their parents do not care, or that they will judge them, criticize them or tell them what to do. Granted some parents do that, but after reading so many wonderful books, I realize that our relationship can be so much better if I just listen to you. If you ever want me to help you create a solution, just let me know."

Curious about her behavior, Val pondered, "I wonder why Tempest is so mean to everyone."

"That's a good question. Something in her life is causing her to lash out at others. She must be angry or upset about something and more than likely is really suffering as a result. It must be difficult for her to look into a mirror and be happy with her life and herself."

A large bang caused them both to jump, as Al and Reese barreled through the kitchen door. Al asked, "Are we ready to eat yet? We're both starving."

After lunch, Al looked up at the sky. "It looks like we'll get some rain today. We better get busy." Reese and his dad went to work putting the final repairs on the tree house that Grandpa Henry had made for the kids.

Reese thought about the incident that had caused the damage to the tree house. His dad had agreed to let Reese and some older boys play in the tree house – boys Reese wanted to impress. However, the older boys ended up trying to break the boards and branches and even threw things at the robin's nest that was perched outside the window.

That is when he had seen his little sister watching them with big tears streaming down her face. Reese felt terrible.

Thinking back to another time, he remembered his grandpa being so proud of what they had created. They spent many nights creating a perfect hideaway from the world.

"I'm sorry, Dad, that you have to go through all this work to fix our tree house. I guess my choice of friends wasn't so hot."

His dad tried to ease the pain. "It's sometimes hard to control how other people act."

"Well I'm making a pact with you to only invite my favorite friends back — those who respect other people's property."

"You just said a very powerful word Reese … respect. Wouldn't it be great if everyone respected each other and each other's property? We would live in a world where we would never have to lock anything. Just imagine the impact that would make!"

"Yeah -- jiiT-Now!"

"What was that you said?"

"jiiT-Now. Val taught a word me. It means 'just imagine it now'. It's kind of like saying 'cool' but it's even better."

"Well I'll be. I suppose we can make up words – after all someone did many years back. That Val, she sure does have a creative mind!"

Just then, Jean came out of the house. "Reese, before we go into town, you need to start packing for your Boy Scout camp-out on Monday night. When we get back, it will be time for bed – so it's best to get it done now."

"Yeah I will. I just need to make sure that I have batteries for my flashlight. I know that morning will come fast."

That evening the Flick family went back into town to visit and grill supper with some friends in the park. Reese and the other boys started to form teams for a softball game.

"Can I play, too?" Val was used to being included in Reese's plans.

Before Reese could respond, one of the boys blurted out, "No. You're a girl!"

Reese explained. "Val, it would be nice if we could all play together, but tonight it's just us boys." Reese gave her the I'm-sorry-and-I'll-make-it-up-to-you-later look.

Val was disappointed. "That's okay; I really didn't want to play." Perking up she added, "Anyway I want to go visit Betty." As she walked away, she realized how Sally must have felt when Tempest was teasing her. Just as Val was thinking of Tempest, she was surprised to look up and see her entering the store.

Tempest strutted up to Betty and said snidely, "Hi, I'm Tempest, Val's new friend."

Somewhat taken back, Betty responded, "Well – it's nice to meet some of Val's friends."

Tempest looked at Betty's right foot wrapped in an ace bandage. "What did you do to your foot?"

"Oh, I twisted my ankle this morning as I stepped off the ladder."

Not acknowledging Betty's explanation, a devilish look came over Tempest's face and she blurted out, "Well, I would like to buy some candy."

Betty had no reason not to trust a girl who claimed to be a friend of Val's. "You just go behind the counter – and bring me what you want to buy. Then you can pay me right here."

Just as Tempest turned to go to the candy aisle, Val walked into the store.

"Hello Betty!"

Tempest stopped Val before she could make it too far into the store. "Stay there and we'll pick out some candy." Walking toward Val, Tempest turned Val around with a swing of her arm and whispered "Remember when I gave you candy? Well, now it is payback time. Come with me." They walked behind the counter. "Here, put this licorice in your pants." Tempest shoved a small bag at her.

Val, looking puzzled, did as Tempest told her as she shoved the candy down her pants. She knew it was not right. She knew she could never tell her parents or anyone else for that matter. That same sick feeling started in her stomach and she felt very bad about what she just did.

"Now let's tell Betty that we're going outside to play in the park — and I'll go pay for this." She held out a few pieces of candy and gave Val a big shove toward the door.

"Ba-bye Betty — I'll see you later. I guess we're going to swing for a while." Val stammered as she walked outside in a daze.

Tempest paid for the candy that was in her hand, spun around and walked away. "Have a good night."

Meanwhile, Betty could not help but look at the girl suspiciously, sensing something was not right. "What did she say to Val to get her to go outside with her?" she thought to herself. Betty got up and hobbled over to the window to watch the girls run to the swings in the park. At that moment, she saw Val pull the licorice out of her pants. A large tear ran down Betty's face as she turned away.

Before they even reached the swings, Val shoved the candy at

Tempest. "Here, I don't want any of this."

Tempest grabbed it out of her hand.

Not knowing what else to say, Val grabbed one of the swings and started swinging as if she were alone. It was starting to rain and everyone scrambled to get into their cars.

Tempest was chattering about something as Val saw the family car pull up to the edge of the park. Thankful to have a good reason to leave, she jumped off the swing. "Bye, I have to go home now." She quickly ran to the car.

That night, Val tossed and turned in her bed and finally sat straight up just as a loud clap of thunder sounded. She crawled out of bed and quietly tip toed down the stairs. She could hear her mom and dad talking about something they called "options" and the tone of their voices did not sound good to Val.

She heard her dad say, "Our land is right where Mr. Matador wants to build storage units. That means he is not going to give up until he forces us to sell those acres. Unfortunately, he is leaving us no room to say no. I'm just going to have to try and talk to him again."

Val crept back up the stairs and went to her room. Worried about the conversation she just heard, she sat on the window bench hugging her legs close to her chest. Looking out into the black night, she wondered how, after stealing the candy, she could ever look Betty in the face again.

A slim, silver moon barely lit up the night and the family home was nestled in the midst of darkness. Their quaint, modest home had been in the family for three generations. The home had witnessed births, graduations, confirmations, card parties, weddings, and the passing of the older generations. Now it sounded like their property was right in the site of Mr. Matador's next project. Val crawled back into bed and fell asleep. The dark sky was circling above, with lightning cutting across the sky just as a light rain began to fall.

Chapter 5
The First Day of School

"Good morning! It's time to get up." Jean was cheery as she opened the curtains in Val's room. "It's your first day of school as a sixth grader. It rained last night, so you'll have to watch for mud puddles today."

"Morning mom," Val mumbled as she stretched, climbed out of bed and put on her new school clothes.

"When you're done getting dressed, come down and I'll show you the flowers that I picked for your teachers," her mother added as she left the room.

Reese and Val appeared in the kitchen at the same time -- just as Jean plopped a waffle on each of their plates. "Here, you need protein too, so be sure to eat at least one slice of meat or an egg. As soon as you are done, you should brush your teeth."

"I hope you have fun at your Boy Scout camp-out," Val managed to say after swallowing her last bite.

"It should be fun, and it might rain. However, you know our

motto . . . 'be prepared'."

The duo rinsed their dishes off, put them in the dishwasher and giggled as they chased each other up the stairs to finish getting ready for school.

"Val! Reese! Hurry up. I'd like a picture of you before the bus gets here." Jean was always making sure she had the camera handy. After posing for several pictures to make sure their mother had one for the album, Val and Reese heard the bus pull in. They hugged their mother good-bye and she added tearfully, "Have a great first day. I love you both."

"We love you too," the pair said in unison. The bus came and they waved good-bye as they climbed onto it. The driver greeted them both, made sure they were sitting with their seat belts fastened and continued the route. Excited chatter filled the bus as the driver continued the routine stops. Soon the driver parked the bus in front of the school and the children climbed off. Val stood at the bottom of the steps looking up at the impressive school and felt a sense of excitement for a new school year. "This is going to be a year full of adventure," she thought as she walked into the school.

The children made their way to their respective classrooms. Val found her classroom quickly and walked in as their teacher, Mrs. Rogness, started taking pictures of the students. In a distinguished, yet motherly voice, she proclaimed, "Welcome to the sixth grade. Come on in and line up. We are going to take pictures of everyone and will make a directory. That way it will be easier for us to remember each other's names. We'll also make a collage throughout the year to show all the great things that you'll experience and learn."

Tempest walked into the room and said, "Oh, if it isn't Silly Sally and Dumpy Darcy. Look at those ugly shoes." Tempest was wearing the pink and black sneakers from the front window at Betty's store and she was posing as if to draw attention to her feet. Both Val and Sally had wanted them, but both of their mothers said that they were not very practical.

The morning went fast as Mrs. Rogness went over what the school year would look like. "Okay kids, it's now time to change subjects. Today in health, we won't be using our books." Holding up a jar, she asked, "Does anyone know what these are? Please pass this around so everyone can look at them."

Val raised her hand just as Tommy Anderson did. Mrs. Rogness called on Tommy first. Trying to be funny, he asked, "Is it some type of animal doo-doo?"

The kids started laughing before Mrs. Rogness could reply. "No it is not animal feces. Val, I saw your hand up next. Would you like to guess?"

"Is it some type of soap?" she asked quietly.

Mrs. Rogness replied, "No it's not soap, but that's a good guess." As she turned and walked to the front of the room, Tempest snickered. "Val, you're such a dope. I think I'll call you Dopey Soapy."

Val could hear some of the other kids laugh and she cowered down in her seat.

Mrs. Rogness stepped in. "Children stop. It is fine to guess even when you are wrong. As your teacher, I would rather that you guess and be wrong than not participate in the classroom. Now, let us get back to what is in the jar. This is something that can be cooked and eaten, and be used to make many other things. They are lentils. Sally, can you please hand out these worksheets? The Lentil was one of the first agricultural crops grown more than 8,500 years ago. It is a high protein crop and can be used in soups, stews, casseroles and salad dishes. For organic farmers, a good quality lentil seed does not need to be treated with insecticides or fungicides, because it germinates rapidly and seedlings emerge quickly."

The day passed quickly but not quickly enough for Val. That afternoon when she got home from school, her mom asked, "How was the first day?"

"Terrible!"

Expecting to get a cheerful answer, Jean got up from her baking. "Come sit down and let's talk about it."

Val's mouth started quivering as she blurted out, "I hate Tempest, she's mean and she's nasty."

Val's mom gave her a big squeeze. "Those are some pretty strong words. You may mean that you dislike what she does, but it is hard to hate one of God's creations. We are all perfect in our own way and we do the best we can with what we know. Now tell me, what did Tempest do to make you so upset?"

"I don't want to talk about it now." Val began to cry.

"That's okay … just let me know when you are ready … and we'll talk. It's not good to keep things like this bottled up inside of you." Jean paused before she continued. "Say, I have a great idea, how about we make some caramel apples?"

"Yeah, that would nice." Val looked lovingly at her mother.

Her mom grabbed her hand and said, "But first we need to wash up."

After washing up, Val and her mom removed the wrappers from the caramels and threw them in a bowl to melt in the microwave. After piercing each apple with a stick and dipping them in the caramel, they rolled some in chopped peanuts and left some plain as they placed them on the waxed paper to cool.

"I need to go check on the clothes in the dryer. Why don't you have one our apples?"

"That would be great! Thanks, Mom!"

"Thank-you . . . I really appreciate your help. I'll be back in a few minutes."

Sitting and enjoying her caramel apple, Val glanced out the kitchen window and thought back to when she overheard her parents talking about Mr. Matador. She also remembered hearing the words spoken by some men outside of the church on Sunday. "When his brother arrives in town to work at the new gas station and convenience store, then together with their power and money, they will soon own the entire valley."

Her stomach started to churn at the thought of what the Matador family was doing and how they were treating people.

Outside, the clouds continued to swirl and force their way toward the valley and hills that sheltered the family home. It was as if the clouds felt the same way Val did, that something bad was about to happen.

Chapter 6
Sweet Dreams?

That night Val lay all snuggled in her bed, thinking about what had happened at school and at the General Store. Most on her mind was how cruel Tempest was to her and her friends. "What would cause her to be so mean? Every time I'm around her I feel like I'm going to get sick," she whispered to herself.

On the horizon, dark, dangerous and wildly moving clouds were making their way toward Val's home. The summer breeze that came through her window screen seemed to be cooling down quickly. She tossed and turned, and had just fallen asleep when a loud clap of thunder sounded and the wind blew the screen off her window. Large drops of rain started to fall into her room.

Val crawled out of her bed to shut the window. Something caught her eye and she saw her white angora cat scamper across the yard to a tree. "How did you get out of the house Snowball?" She recalled the day that they picked up the kitten from the local Humane Society. Val instantly loved the ball of fur with one blue eye and one green eye. This tiny white ball simply had to be named Snowball. Starting to walk to Reese's room for help, Val remembered that he was at a Boy Scout camp-out. Talking aloud to no one, Val muttered, "Boy, I'll bet they really hate this weather right now." Val wandered to her mom and dad's room to ask them for help. She knocked on the door, even though it was open. She peeked in only to see that their bed was made and her parents were nowhere in sight. She walked down the creaky stairwell. Looking around the entire house, she could not find her parents. She was starting to get scared. With her pajamas damp from nervous perspiration, Val stepped out onto the porch and yelled. "Mom? Dad?" She could not wait any longer, as the wind was starting to pick up even more. She ran down the steps and out into the dark night to rescue her cat from the storm. She yelled into the wind, "Snowball, here kitty, kitty, kitty."

Swirling clouds were everywhere. Like a thick fog, they surrounded her, lifting her up. The fog wrapped around her and she could no longer see anything but the dark gray wall that enveloped her. She felt that she was going higher and higher. The spinning felt more like floating on a raft in a raging river. Val felt oddly warm, but she was scared. She wanted to be home with her mother and father and her little 'Snowball'. She started sobbing uncontrollably. It was as if she was on the worst ride of her life. The storm raged on and on as rain fell harder and harder. Val felt herself being lifted and could see the tops of trees. Everything became a blur and she could no longer make out anything in the darkness. Soon the spinning seemed to slow down, then thump — she landed on a damp, yet pleasantly warm area. The thick fog seemed to warm her like the fleece blanket she had on her bed. As she attempted to sit up, heaviness overwhelmed her and she fell back into an exhausting sleep.

Chapter 7
Up Above the Clouds

As Val started to wake up, she could hear low, whispering voices.

One voice giggled. "Tee hee, should we wake her, or let her sleep? Oh, she looks just like an angel."

A deeper voice responded, "She's not an angel — but she is something just as important!"

"What do you mean?" Val heard the other voice ask. She stirred slightly so she could better hear the faint voices talking back and forth. She wanted to wake up but felt so drowsy and comfortable. Not quite ready to wake from this dream, she laid there listening.

The deep voice responded emphatically, "She's Val — she represents 'values' and what is right and good with mankind!"

"Mankind?" the softer voice asked.

The deep voice replied, "Yes, you know, the ones who live down there — on earth."

Wanting to get a closer look at this little girl who seemed to have great importance, the other character moved quickly in front of her.

Val, still shaking off the cobwebs in her head, sat up and tried to open her eyes. As she struggled to keep them open against the bright light, she noticed someone – or something — right in front of her face peering over her. The fluffy, white figures looked like clouds, but maybe they were giant marshmallows like those that Reese had teased her about that day on the hill. On the other hand, maybe they were giant cotton balls. Both of them were so transparent and wispy. "It can't be possible." Val rubbed her eyes. "I must be dreaming," she muttered to herself as she fainted and fell back into the puffy whiteness.

What Val saw was the real thing. The two cloud characters who enveloped the area where she lay – really were alive and were actually talking with her.

"Honesty, I can't believe what you just did," said the deeper voiced cloud puff. "Can't you see that you scared her and she fainted?"

Honesty backed away from the sleeping girl. "No, I didn't. I was only trying to get a closer look at her and show her a friendly face when she woke up!"

"Well, did you ever stop to think that she may be scared of us and what we look like?" asked the puff of cloud named Integrity.

Val started to stir again. She sat up and stretched out her arms, yawning. "Where am I?" She looked around and noticed the cottony cloud people. "Who are you?"

"Hi — I'm Honesty! But my family calls me Esty." one of the puffy people said matter-of-factly.

The other figure stated in a forceful, deep voice. "I'm In-teg-rity. The relatives call me Teg for short. Do not be afraid, Val. We're here to take care of you."

Val was puzzled. "How did you know my name?"

"Well, we know everything that happens down there," Esty replied.

"What do you mean down there?" asked Val, looking down. She started to stand in a transparent film of clouds. "Whoa, I'm going to fall."

"No, you won't fall. It's impossible, until things change — and do we mean change!" said Esty.

Teg took Val by the hand. "Come with us and we'll show you." They jumped from cloud to cloud, until they came to an opening. Val was starting to like these two characters. Besides, she finally got to feel what it was like to walk in the clouds. Starting to relax, Val giggled as they hopped from a large cloudbank to an even larger one. "I've always wanted to do this, but didn't think it was possible." The trio jumped onto the next large cloud, sliding down as if it were a long, winding slide. Val felt so light and peaceful as they continued jumping and sliding – until all of a sudden they came to a stop. They softly bumped into each other as if they were large stuffed pillows. They stood at the edge of the lowest cloud formation.

Teg pointed downward. "See those hills and that stream of water? Look closer; see the dog running in the yard?"

"That's what we mean by down there," Esty added softly.

"Oh, there's my house and my dad. He's picking up what looks like tree branches. He must not be working today. Otherwise he would be at work by now." Becoming even more excited, Val yelled,

"Dad," as loud as she could. She shot a pleading look at Esty, "Look, he's upset." She watched him throw the branches onto a trailer as if he were mad at each and every stick of wood.

"It's no use, Val ... he can't hear you." Esty looked right at Val. "Do you realize that you and Tempest did a very bad thing? You stole from someone ... and it was even someone who loves you."

Val looked sad. "Oh ... you must mean Betty."

Esty and Teg looked at her solemnly and both nodded.

Without hesitation, Teg added, "But ... you have a chance to turn things around — through Tempest!"

"Through Tempest?" Val asked, looking disgusted.

Teg looked down through the clouds. "Even though everyone can change, it seems that younger people are more open and can adjust more quickly. Especially when they realize how much better they will feel when they treat people well."

Esty started swirling around and flinging her wispy arms. "You really hurt Betty's feelings. Did you know she watched you and Tempest through the window? She saw you pull the candy out of your clothes ... she was so crushed. She loves you very much. Do you remember the surprise birthday party she threw for you in the back of her store? Betty has loved you like you were her own ... and you stole from her."

Val's eyes welled up with tears.

Teg interrupted. "Esty, stop it. You're making her cry!"

"But I'm just being honest. Besides crying can help get it out of your system. I also want to add that being honest hurts less in the long run."

Teg could not help but jump in. "Don't you know that since she's human she sometimes needs to make mistakes – just so she can learn from them?"

Esty, still pacing, proclaimed, "That's cow manure and a bad excuse — it's insanity. People only came up with the saying, 'I'm only human' ... ha ha ha ... just to make themselves feel better when they know they purposely did something wrong. That statement should only count when it's an honest mistake and not done on purpose. Val could have controlled what she did, so that means there is no excuse or reason for her doing it. Okay, so answer me this: since she represents values, does that mean that she now gets punished?"

"Not exactly — it's actually better," said Teg. "She not only gets to learn from her mistake but she will help make a difference in someone else's life. All of this before she can go home again."

Val looked worried. "What do you mean, before I can go home again?"

"First things first," stated Teg. The big puffy cloud looked very somber and continued slowly. "Having integrity is becoming more difficult everyday for the human race. It makes me very sad because you humans believe in me less and less ... just like faith stops existing once you do not believe anymore. Look at the world and the crime ... the pollution, drugs and gangs. Worse yet, see how they treat themselves ... and each other." Teg paused, took a deep breath and then proclaimed, "Val ... you ... you can make a difference."

"You can and you will make a difference," Esty added. "You can add 'value' to the lives of those who know you. Just as we need to add more caring, concern and love to mankind... but that will come later. You will help them to see that to live a fulfilling life, they need to change and let go of their past mistakes and bad behavior. So first, we need to deal with the matter at hand."

Val thought for a moment and then interrupted. "Okay. Stop. Before we go any farther… you have to tell me what your definition of integrity is."

"You bring up a good point," said Teg, realizing the importance of Val's inquest. "Integrity means that you actually do what you say you are going to do when you say you will. Therefore, if you tell your mom that you will clean your room by 10:00 a.m. – then you really do clean it by 10:00 a.m.! It is about keeping your word and about doing the right thing without people even asking you to. If you do not keep your word, it is also important to clear the air with the other person. That way you will both feel complete. I would sum it up by saying six simple words: 'Honor your self. Honor your word.' "

Chapter 8
The Calm after the Storm

The TV was on in the background as Val's mother tried to stay busy. She was not paying attention as the news anchor told about the effects of last night's storm. The news anchor was saying, "The County is cleaning up after one of the worst wind storms to hit our area in years. Straight-line winds of 90 mph tore through the entire area. Many homes suffered damage; fortunately, no lives were lost. However, eleven-year-old Val Flick, daughter of Al and Jean Flick, of Manfred is missing. There are search parties out and will continue until dark. You can help by calling 555-777-HELP. Again the number is 555-777-HELP."

Jean wanted to be home in case anyone called or if Val came home. She picked up yesterday's mail from the counter and looked at the letter her husband had opened earlier. As she read the letter, she realized why Al had seemed upset when he read it. She gasped and heard herself say aloud to no one, "Dear God, Al hasn't heard from his father in over twenty years." Jolted back to reality by the phone ringing, she wondered how it was going at the school as she rushed to pick it up.

Meanwhile, the children were arriving at the school. There was a lot of whispering going on that something had happened to Val Flick. One of the older boys had overheard the teachers talking and rushed to share what he had heard. The warning bell rang and everyone settled into their classrooms. They all anxiously waited for Mrs. Rogness to start the class. She softly said, "Good morning class. I have some information to share with you. This morning Val's parents discovered that sometime during the night she left their house. They are not sure if she ran outside to bring her cat in, or what happened to her. With the rain and wind last night, she could have looked to find shelter somewhere else. Today we are going to dismiss classes to help support the search efforts for Val. The city is coordinating the search and all of your parents agreed to let you help in different ways. Those who are organizing the search will talk to you about your specific task when we are done with class. We also have Ms. Neilson, the school counselor, in our class to talk with us before we dismiss."

The counselor stood up and greeted the class. "Good morning. I am very glad to be here to talk with you about what you may be feeling because of Val's disappearance. It is important for you to know that her parents believe that she is safe and alive. It is normal to feel sad . . . and many of you will be concerned and worried until you hear what has happened to her. I encourage you to talk about it with each other and your parents, since talking about it will make you feel better. You are always welcome to visit with me at any time."

"Thank you Ms. Neilson," said Mrs. Rogness. "Okay class . . . it's time to dismiss. If your parents are not outside waiting for you, go ahead and get on one of the buses. Rather than taking you home, the buses will stop at the park where you will find out what you can do to help. Let's make the most of today and I'll see you back in class tomorrow morning."

The children quietly started filing out of the room. Some of the girls stopped to look at the collage of pictures Mrs. Rogness had taken just the day before. As the girls looked over the pictures, they started to cry.

Tempest rolled her eyes. "Quit being such babies. Val deserved everything she got."

"Val is a good person!" Sally snapped back at her. "She doesn't deserve this. Val is nice to everyone."

Another friend, Marcia, blurted out, "Yeah, Val is nice to everyone!"

Tempest mimicked them in a nasty way. "Oh, Val is nice to everyone," she smirked as she left the room laughing to herself. "Well at least we get out of school."

Most of the parents were waiting to pick up their kids and the remaining students boarded the bus for a ride to the search area. They would create a plan for all of them to help.

The bus that carried the Boy Scout troop was just pulling up in front of the school. It had engine problems and the troop was late in returning. Val's dad had been anxiously waiting for the bus to arrive.

As Reese got off the bus with his friends, he looked up and saw his dad. "What are you doing here?"

"Reese we need to talk. Last night in the storm . . . Val must have run outside." Al paused and took a deep breath. "There is no sign of her and people are saying that with the bad storm, if she was outside, she may not have survived."

Reese, visibly shaken by his dad's news, blurted out "No way, I don't believe for one minute that she is dead. She can't be and I won't believe it!" he said as he choked back the tears. "Let's go, we have to look for her."

"Your mother and I believe that she's okay. We've been looking for her since we woke up this morning and we'll keep searching until we find her," Al said tiredly. "We need to stick together now more than ever." Al gave Reese a hug. "Let's go – everyone who can help is gathering at the park. "Your mom is at home in case anyone calls or if Val comes home."

Reese threw his things in the trunk and they got into the car to start the search. Reese still did not believe what he had heard. "Why? Why would Val run outside?"

"We don't know Son but we will find her. She could have been chasing after that darn cat again. The minute that I opened the door this morning, it came tearing into the house. We checked on her last night before we went to the basement to move some boxes in case the sump pump failed. She was in her bed, sound asleep."

Both men were lost in their thoughts as they drove until Reese broke the silence. "Dad, if we don't find her by dark, is it okay if I set up the tent outside and wait there in case she comes back?"

"I'm sure Val would like that." They arrived at the park, where the community and National Guard were gathering.

Sally and her family walked over to the Flick's car. "Don't worry, we're going to find Val and we're all here to help," Sally said confidently.

The crowd began to quiet down as Mayor Beilke gave instructions. "Good morning. First, thank you all for coming out to help. We have an important task ahead of us and it is time to get started. Second, we are forming teams to search the area. If you find her or see anything that looks suspicious, call out or use your cell phone to call 555-776-1287. Most of the men will be checking the woods and along the river. Some of the women and children will stay behind in the shelter or will go to the Flick home to be with Jean in case Val returns home. For those staying here, we have supplies and photos to make posters. Some of you could help by making food and having it ready for throughout the day. We also need some of you to walk through the entire town. It will be important to go to every house, look in every tree grove and every building. She may have found a place out of the storm and fallen asleep. If we do not see you the rest of the day, we will keep meeting back here every morning until Val is home. Good luck everyone and be safe out there."

Through the window of the General Store, Betty watched a vintage Mercedes car pull up. She was disappointed that she could not help search for Val, but someone had to stay back and keep the store open in case anyone needed supplies. As she walked behind the counter, lost in thoughts about Val, she looked up to see a distinguished looking man get out of the car and hurriedly make his way into the store.

"Excuse me," he said.

As she started to greet him, their eyes locked. The man hesitated briefly, and then continued. "I'm looking for a nice bouquet of flowers or a plant. It has been many years since I have seen my son and I would like to make a good impression on him and his family.

Betty, surprised by her instant attraction to the man, stepped forward to direct him to the plants and flowers. It was as if she were floating above watching a movie with two people having a conversation.

He reached for a colorful pot, "This plant looks good. The tag lists this as mums. The word is certainly fitting for me, as I've been gone a long time with no contact at all."

"If you don't mind me asking, who are you going to see? I know most everyone and could perhaps make a suggestion for you."

"I'm off to see Al Flick and his family."

"Oh yes, I know them very well. I believe they would all enjoy this large bouquet of mums. Before you leave, I should let you know some important news about Al's little girl, Val. She is missing…disappeared earlier today. Al and the search team are at McBain Park." Dabbing her eyes with a tissue, she continued. "I really do care for Val and love her like she is my own. You should go there, as I'm sure they would really appreciate your help."

The man tipped his hat to Betty. "That is exactly what I'll do." After paying for the plant, he started to leave and then turned back with a sudden look of recognition. "Betty, little Betty Berndt — is that you? It has to be you! I would have thought with all of your traveling and adventures that you would have never returned to Manfred."

"Yes it is me; but we can catch up later. She walked Al's father to the door, realizing that she did remember him from many years back.

"Much obliged. I would like to thank you properly but I should go and help. Perhaps I can take you out for dinner sometime after Val is home safe and sound."

He turned toward the door as Betty quietly answered. "That would be wonderful." She walked to the window and watched the man walk away. Never in her life had she felt so stirred with emotion. She shook her head and turned away as if to deny her feelings. "What has gotten into you Betty — my word — it's not as if you've never seen a man before!" However, she knew this one was special. She could not wait to see the 'familiar stranger' again.

Chapter 9
Someone to Watch over Me

Val started to tear up as she watched the commotion going on. "I miss Reese. What about him? Can I go see him? You must know how much I miss him! If you have brothers and sisters, you would miss them too. Please!

"No, you can't see him right now — and yes, we do have brothers and sisters." Esty started to list their names. "There is Patience and Trust. Kindness and Respect — who are off on a world tour. Then there is Courage, Faith, Humility and Belief. We also have lots of other cousins and relatives. So, we really do know how much you miss Reese." Esty paused. "Hey Teg, should we tell her about Reese?"

"This is as good a time as any." Teg took a deep breath and continued. "We have something very important to tell you about your brother. Reese represents responsibility on earth. Without it, our world would crumble. Everyone needs to be responsible for what they say and do. We see people everyday making choices that hurt others and even themselves. They just need to think before doing."

Esty added, "I've heard so many people say, 'I didn't think about that.' Just like the babysitter, we were watching last week. She stepped away from the changing table and the baby rolled off. Luckily, the baby rolled onto a bed and only scratched its arm on a toy that was on the bed. Being responsible, she told the parents. However, she was not being responsible when she stepped away. There was also the kid who lost his lunch money by not being responsible for the location of it. There are lots of examples."

Val puffed up her chest proudly. "I always knew Reese was special." As she looked down through the clouds, she saw something that made her cry out in frustration. "Oh, there she is!" Esty and Teg followed Val's pointed finger and saw Tempest enter the General Store.

Tempest blurted out to Betty, "My mother sent me to buy some apples." After grabbing two bags and plopping them in front of Betty, she stood and stared blankly at her.

Betty nodded and rang them up. She thanked Tempest and turned away, not able to look at the girl.

As Tempest left the store, she slipped a flat item into her bag. She muttered quietly, "That was easy! Betty sure wasn't thinking when she put the Halloween display table by the door." She snickered to herself and started to walk home. The closer she got to her house, the madder she got as she muttered to herself: "I'm sure everyone is looking for Val, and now I'm stuck baking apple pies with my mom for the search party." Tempest was frustrated as she walked into the house. She kicked Lady, their Portuguese water dog out of a nice nap. Took its chew toy and put it up on the table. "Now just try and get it," she muttered as the dazed dog looked up at her quizzically.

She put the apples on the counter, completely ignoring her mother and Marion their housekeeper. Not wanting to help in any way, she did not respond when her mother said, "Marion and I could really use some help in peeling these apples."

Disregarding her mother, she walked into the family room where her little brother Matt was watching TV. Tempest plopped down on the couch, grabbed the remote control and turned the channel as Matt cried out, "Hey, I was watching that."

Tempest shot back snidely, "I know, but now I'm watching TV."

"Why do you have to be so mean to me all the time?" Matt yelled back.

"Well little brother, because a 'mat' is something you walk all over." She stood up and started prancing around the room, stomping on the area rug singing, "Matt, Matt the rubber mat, walk on him and he'll never fight back."

Matt started crying, turned, and ran out of the room.

Chapter 10
Back to the Search

The stranger walked up to the crowd that had gathered by the shelter in McBain Park. He immediately recognized his son talking with a police officer.

Al had sensed something. He stopped talking and turned his head toward his father in disbelief. The two men walked toward each other and as they met, each stopped, not knowing what to do next. They stared at each other in silence for what seemed like an eternity.

Ray broke the silence. "Son, I just heard what happened and I came to help out."

Al replied blankly. "I'm grateful. We can use all the help we can get." He turned and started walking back to the group.

Running to catch up with him, Ray said, "Al, I know it has been years and I know that I shouldn't have left Manfred after your mother divorced me, but I knew you'd be better off without me. I realize you're busy right now, but I want to explain to you what happened."

Al turned toward his father and said angrily, "I know Dad, I'm sure you had your reasons, but that doesn't mean that you fall off the earth for twenty years of my life." He turned away. "Dad, right now all I care about is finding my daughter."

The search parties looked until it was too dark, and then finished up with a warm meal. Al stood in front of the group. "Thanks to each and every one of you. I don't know what we would do if we didn't have such great friends. You all seem to understand that when something happens to someone that you love, nothing else matters. Not the crops, not work, not money and certainly not sleep."

The crowd nodded agreements to each other. Al continued. "For those of you who can make it, we're going to start again in the morning. It looks like it may rain again, so let's plan to meet in the church at 7:00 a.m. We will have a hot breakfast before we get started – thanks to the Ladies Aid. Thank you all again and have a good night."

Tired from the search and saddened by the lack of any clues, the searchers walked to their cars in silence.

Gene, a life-long friend of the family, walked over to Al. "Some of us have brought tents, and we are going to join you for the night. We can take turns keeping the fire burning, and we'll start the search with you in the morning."

Al looked up at the bright moon. Whenever he looked at clouds, he felt a calming effect come over him. "The strangest thing about this, Gene, is that I know she's okay. I don't know where she is, but I just have a feeling that she is in good hands."

Gene put his arm around Al's shoulder. "I agree. Don't worry, Al – we're going to find her soon."

Chapter 11
A Skeleton in the Closet

That night in her room, Tempest was planning to use the package she had stolen from Betty's Halloween display to scare her younger brother. She thought to herself, "I'll wait until Matt goes to bed, then I'll give him the scare of his life." When she heard him go into the bathroom, she grabbed the glow-in-the-dark skeleton that was charging by her light, and quietly crept into his room. She put the skeleton into his closet and ran back to her room to wait.

Only a thin wall separated the two closets. It would be easy for her to bang on the wall and make her brother think that there was something in his closet. She knocked and ran back to bed, snickering proudly to herself. Soon she heard the creak of her brother's closet door. Then she heard a scream. Matt's bedroom door flew open and she could hear him running down the hall to find his parents. Tempest ran into his room. As she grabbed the skeleton, she stepped in something wet. "Oh, for disgusting, the jerk peed in his pants." Back in her room, she hid the skeleton behind her dresser and crawled back into bed — pretending to sleep.

She could hear her parents go into his room with him as he tried to explain that something was in his closet. They finally got him settled down by pretending to chase all of the bad things out of his room and out of the house. Tempest soon heard her mother and father leaving his room.

Tempest laughed herself to sleep feeling very proud that she had scared her brother so much that he actually peed in his pants. "The little jerk deserved it," she thought to herself as she fell asleep.

Chapter 12
Time to Go to Work

Teg, with a determined look on his face proclaimed, "It's time to teach Tempest a lesson I don't mean that in a bad way, but in a way that she can learn from her mistakes."

Esty turned to Val. "Val, you are on this earth for a reason, and you need to know that everything happens for a reason. It's now time for you to help teach Tempest."

"You can and will make a difference – that is who you are, someone who will make a difference," she continued. "We can place you anywhere we want to and we can bring you back as quick as you can say 'please'. 'Please' is such a simple word, and it has so much power.

Teg added, "It's important for you to remember that until things start to change, the only person who can see you is Tempest."

Val scrunched up her nose in protest. "Tempest, oh no, do I have to? She's so mean to me."

"Get with it, girl. You gotta do what you gotta do. Now let's get down to work." Esty placed her puffy cloud hand on Val's shoulder.

"Now it is up to you," added Teg. "Are you ready?"

Back at the park, it had grown dark. Ray walked over to Al. "Son, do you think we can talk now?"

In a tired voice Al replied, "Well actually Ray, I need you to go back to the General Store and buy some matches, so we can restart the fire if it goes out. Do you know the way?"

"Yes I do. I stopped there earlier."

"I'd appreciate it since we used the last matches starting this fire. Besides, I'm not in the mood to get into a conversation with you yet." Al turned and walked away.

Ray walked to his car with his head down, but as soon as he remembered where he was going, he felt uplifted. As he drove toward the store, he muttered to himself, "I can't remember the last time a woman made me feel interested. I wonder what it is about her." As he pulled up to the store, he saw the lights go off. He quickly jumped out of the car and ran to the door. He tapped lightly. Soon the outdoor light went back on.

Betty opened the door and was surprised to see the 'familiar stranger' standing in front of her.

"Don't you know it's unsafe to open a door not knowing who is on the other side?" he teased.

Betty laughed. "Well, in Manfred we've never had to worry about it. Come on in, before all the bugs do."

Ray stepped in and Betty reached beyond him to shut off the outside light. He sniffed the air. "Is that pumpkin pie I smell?"

Betty turned in surprise and stammered, "Well, yes, it is."

"I knew it. I have a nose that doesn't miss anything that smells that delicious." Ray seemed to forget why he had come to the store. "I love the smell of home baked desserts. For that matter, I love the smell of any home cooked meal."

Realizing that she did not really know the person who seemed like an old lost friend, Betty stuck out her hand. "Let's re-introduce ourselves. Hello, I'm Betty, what's your name?"

Startled back to reality, Ray answered, embarrassed. "I'm sorry, I forgot my manners. I am Ray, Ray Flick. I'm Al Flick's father." His voice fell. "I'm sure you haven't heard of me."

"No, I can't say that I have," Betty answered. "I assumed both of Al's parents had passed away because he never talked about you. But I do remember seeing your face around town many years ago."

"Yes, I can't say I'm proud of being gone for so long. But I had my reasons."

Betty changed the subject. "Well, what brings you here tonight?"

Betty's question brought Ray back to the reality of the situation. "I came to get some matches."

Betty turned and walked to the back of the store. "The matches are back here. Follow me."

As Betty walked to the back of the store, Ray could not help but notice her silhouette. She walked with a feminine dignity he had never seen.

Betty stopped and turned around, almost running into Ray. "Where are you from that you don't feel safe opening a door when someone knocks?"

"Manhattan — the city that never sleeps."

"Oh, now that brings back memories. I remember my father taking me to the Statue of Liberty when I was fourteen. I loved the ferry ride and the seagulls."

"You've been there?" Ray was surprised.

"I've been fortunate enough to have traveled many places," added Betty. "My aunt and uncle tended the store as my father and I traveled each summer. One of my favorite photos that I have is of the Twin Towers taken on the ferry ride back from Liberty Island. God bless those who lost their lives and those who have suffered from 9/11. It was a terrible tragedy."

She stopped in front of a shelf, pointing, "Well, here are the matches."

Ray picked up a box. "Thanks." Not ready to leave yet, he added, "You wouldn't happen to have a cup of tea or anything to take off a chill?"

Betty was happy that Ray wanted to stay. "As a matter of fact, I had started the tea kettle right before I shut the lights off. Come with me — you can have a cup of tea and a piece of pie."

Betty invited Ray through the store and to the back screened in porch where they sat on the chair swing watching the clouds move through the crescent moon. After a few minutes, Ray remembered the park – and Al. "That was excellent pie, Betty. Thank you. I really should be getting back to the park. I am hoping my son and I have a chance to make up for lost time. I was not a good father to him, and now I regret it. I left his mom and him to go to New York for a job." Betty looked at him sadly, as he continued. "I was stubborn and thought I could rule her and the world. Then it was too late. She divorced me and got custody of our son."

"And you haven't seen him since?"

"Oh I did — he just didn't know it," Ray replied sadly. "Once I came back on the train to see him at the Christmas play, but I couldn't bring myself to let people know I was here. I dressed up as an elf and handed out candy bags after the program. I guess I lost my nerve. I caught an early train and went back to New York. I also came home for his graduation, but was lost in the crowd. I approached him, but he turned away from me. I told myself he did not see me. I could not bear to talk to him, so I left. Next, I heard that he had graduated from college and was getting married. I kept track of him by subscribing to the local paper. I saw that he had two children and was named Postmaster at the Manfred Post Office. I was so proud of him and all that he did for the community, but I knew he didn't want to see me. One of the saddest days was when my Gena passed away. It broke my heart that I never made it up to her." He wiped away a tear. "I can only pray that it's not too late for my son and me."

After several minutes of silence, Betty said, "I've known Al since he was a child. He has a big heart and I'm sure after he hears what you have to say, he'll forgive you."

Ray looked hopeful. "There's a lot more to it, but I guess that's something I should talk about with Al."

Betty stood as if urging him to leave. "Well, I think it's time that you do that." She started walking toward the door.

"You're right, Betty." They walked back into the store and made their way to the entrance.

Ray said softly, "After this is over, I would like to get to know you better. Do you mind if I stop for tea again?"

Flashing him a reassuring smile, Betty replied, "I would enjoy that. Have a good night."

He reached out for her hand and kissed the top of it. "Thanks for the nice chat. I now know what I have to say to Al. Good night. I will see you tomorrow."

"Good night," Betty replied as he walked out and shut the door.

Ray turned the car around and headed back to the park, smiling for the first time in many years. When he got to the four-way stop, he looked up and watched the Northern Lights as they danced in the sky. Feeling a sense of peace, he looked forward to getting back to Al.

Chapter 13
Knock Knock

The rest of the Matador family had all gone to bed, but Tempest could not stop thinking about everything that was going on in town. As she tossed, turned, and listened to the wind outside, she finally fell into a restless sleep.

Sometime during the middle of the night, Val appeared in Tempest's closet. Val was glad the night light in Tempest's room allowed enough light underneath the door so she could see where she was. The house was quiet. Val looked around the closet, "These are the pink and black sneakers that Tempest wore the first day of school. The ones she bragged about when she was teasing Sally and Darcy." They were the same pair that Val had wanted. She looked around at all Tempests' fancy things. Among the many toys and games, Val saw a doll that had its arm ripped off. Another's hair was all matted and an eye was missing. "Tempest must have never taken care of anything. If I had such beautiful dolls, I would treasure them." Startled back to reality, she remembered the rotten plot that Tempest had just imposed on her younger brother. Val tapped on the closet door.

Tempest jolted awake and sat up in bed. Startled, she thought to herself, "I know that can't be Matt, he isn't smart enough to get back at me." She heard the tap again, so she threw off the covers and jumped out of bed. As she pulled open the closet door, she saw Val holding one of her dolls. Tempest immediately snatched the doll from Val's hands. "Give me my doll! Uh, eh, uh, Val, Val-l-l, what are you doing? I must be dreaming."

Tempest slammed the door. Val rapped twice but Tempest just stood there.

Val finally said, "Knock-Knock!" Again, silence. Then Val blurted out, "This is when you're supposed to say 'who's there?'"

Tempest slowly opened the door, peering into the closet. Then she instantly slammed it shut and propped the chair against it so Val could not get out. She ran out of her room and down the hall yelling, "Mom, Dad come quick!" Running into their room, she grabbed her dad's arm, pulling him out of bed and dragging him down the hallway. Her mother followed in a daze. On the way back to her room, Tempest was clamoring, "Val is supposed to be dead, but she's not; she's in my closet. Come see."

When they got to her room, Tempest opened the closet door. Val was gone. Tempest, becoming hysterical, screamed out, "She was here, I saw her and I locked her in my closet!"

"Tempest you are always making up stories and we're both too tired to put up with any of them tonight," her dad said tiredly. "The next time you drag us out of bed like this, you will be punished."

"Remember the book about the little boy who cried wolf?"

her mom sighed. "Well maybe we'll have to read that one again. Goodnight sweetheart, we'll see you in the morning."

M. FAYE WATERS

Chapter 14
The Search Continues

"Come on kids, get in the car," boomed Craig Matador. "There's a meeting at the church to talk about the ongoing search for Val Flick, and we need to make our appearance."

As they drove to the church, Esther, whose heart was large enough to make up for her husband's lack of care and concern for others, suggested, "We should make sure that they put up posters in the surrounding cities."

As they pulled up to the church, Craig hissed, "Tempest, because of your prank last night, you can sit in the car until we are ready to go home."

As he turned away, Tempest stuck out her tongue and made a squishy face. "But I'm hungry and I want some breakfast."

Her dad turned around, and glared at her. "Not after the pranks you've been pulling." He turned and walked toward the church with his wife and son.

"I saw what you did," said Val matter-of-factly as she appeared in the seat beside Tempest.

"What are you doing to me? You are dead - did you hear what I said – dead!" yelled Tempest.

"No I'm not! I'm just visiting a better place."

"Okay, like I said — dead!" Tempest was disgusted with Val. "I guess your goody two shoes got you into heaven. So then, stop haunting me and go away."

"I can't," Val stated simply.

"What do you mean you can't?"

"I'm here to show you that life doesn't have to be this way. YOU don't have to be this way."

"What do you mean 'this way'? I have everything I want," Tempest said in a sassy tone of voice. "My parents are rich and everyone in town does what my dad tells them to do. I can do anything and say anything that I want to — like 'GO AWAY!'" Tempest looked away from Val, but out of the corner of her eye she tried to see if Val was still there.

Val shrugged. "I told you that I can't leave." Val looked intently at Tempest. "Can't you just for once try to talk nicely to someone or to do something nice? Just try it — you'll be amazed at how good it will make you feel."

"If my parents see you, this game you are playing is over," Tempest cried.

"They can't see me, only you can." Val continued. "Don't you know that people want to be around people that are nice? You are not a nice person. You tease and hurt people. Don't you want people to love you? Remember your old nanny, Darlene? She loved you very much and really misses you since you moved."

Tempest's face started to soften. "All I ever wanted was for someone to love me."

"Well you sure have a funny way of showing that to people," Val replied softly.

Tempest turned to see the door to the church open and her parents make their way back to the car. "What good does it do when all that ever happens is …" She turned back to Val only to realize she was talking to empty space.

On the drive back to the house, Tempest started thinking about the visit from Val, wondering if it was real. "Maybe Val made sense," she thought to herself. "After all, it seems that everyone avoids me …even the cat and dog. I don't deserve to be loved, I never do anything right. Nobody even likes me."

Chapter 15
Lesson of the Day

The family scattered in different directions for the day. Matt was off to the park, Tempest went to her room to read, Esther went to visit Jean and Craig went to his office. That evening Marion, the housekeeper was busy preparing dinner. Tempest came out of her room and walked into the kitchen and said, "Hi Marion, can I do something to help you?"

Marion looked at Tempest dumbfounded. "Well, yes — you can help set the table."

Tempest looked down at the floor. "I don't really know where you put everything."

"Well it's about time that I show you how to set a proper table." As Marion showed her where to properly place the silverware and dishes, she thought to herself, "The poor girl doesn't even know how to do a simple task." "Tempest, you continue with the glasses and I'll go check on dinner. I don't want to burn anything," she said to the girl.

As Tempest was putting the final glass on the table, she tripped on the carpet and dropped the glass. It hit the hardwood floor and shattered into a hundred pieces.

Her father had just returned from the office and walked into the dining room and seeing the incident yelled, "What do you think you are doing? You have no right helping the employees for what I pay them to do. Now go to your room, I'm tired of your mischief!"

Tempest ran out of the kitchen and upstairs to her room. She threw herself onto her bed, hiding her tearful face in the pillow.

"I'm sorry, Tempest, that your dad yelled at you." Val appeared and sat next to Tempest on the bed. "People's feelings are more important than anything else in the whole world, way more than a silly glass." Val put her hand on Tempest's shoulder. "It is sad that the magic you felt when you were helping Marion was ruined by your father's rudeness. Accidents happen and if other people tried to understand that we don't make or do them on purpose, they wouldn't be so cruel." Attempting to cheer her up, Val started twirling around the room, giggling. "Oh, but what a feeling it is to help someone!"

"You are crazy, and nothing ever changes," Tempest burst out.

"Oh, but it can! It just has to start with you." Val turned on a music box that sat on Tempest's dresser and started twirling around the room. She grabbed Tempest's hands and they started to dance. Tempest felt herself starting to feel happier and more gleeful. She was finally letting down her guard. When the music ended, they sat cross-legged on the floor giggling as they tried to catch their breath.

The tranquility of the moment was interrupted. "Tempest, get down here right now — it's time to eat," yelled her father. Val disappeared as quickly as the laughter on Tempest's face.

As Tempest sadly walked down the massive curving stairway, she could hear her father talking to someone in the foyer. "We'll run them into the ground. If what I told you to do doesn't work, I'm sure you can come up with something to make them sell!" The man left and her dad went to take his seat at the head of the table.

Tempest slowly walked into the dining room, sat down and naively asked, "Father, what does it mean to run someone into the ground?"

"Tempest, when it comes to being successful in business, there can only be one elevator and only one gas station in this town," her father explained. "And we're going to be the one. The sooner these small farmers realize it's time to sell to us, the better for their health."

Tempest started up again, "In school..."

Her dad interrupted with his usual growl. "Sit up to the table."

Tempest continued quietly. "We learned about lentils in school. We found out how healthy they are for your body."

At that moment, her mother and Matt walked into the room and joined them at the table. As if Matt knew it was his turn, he blurted out, "Bless this food, Amen." The family passed the food and began to eat without anyone saying a word.

After a long silence, Tempest finally found the courage to continue, "Dad, about the lentils that Mrs. Rogness told us about... did you know that the climate here is perfect for growing them? Why doesn't Uncle Joe sell the seed and teach people how to grow them? Then we can sell something different than the other elevator instead of running them into the ground."

"Silly girl, what do you know about business!" snorted Craig.

Stuttering and stammering, Tempest blurted out, "I know enough when it sounds like someone is going to be hurt!"

Her father pounded on the table angrily. "That's enough. You either go to your room or go outside and play. I don't want to see your face for the rest of the night."

As Tempest ran from the house, her mother stood up to follow her. Instead of going after her, she clenched her stomach. Her head felt light, everything in the room started to swirl, and then it went black. She fainted, falling back onto her chair.

Chapter 16
All by Myself

Tempest ran out of the house, tears streaming down her face. She slowed to a walk as she approached the park. This park had the same type of slide as the town where they used to live. She remembered how last winter she had wanted to lick the slide as it glistened with a coating of ice. Unfortunately, as she stuck out the tip of her tongue, it stuck to the slide. She felt all alone — just the same as she did that day when no one else was around. She finally built up the courage to pull away. An intense pain had shot through her entire body and her tongue started to throb. She had climbed down from the slide wishing she had not done that. Pushing that dreadful moment from her mind, she grabbed her favorite swing and started to swing as high as she could go. She closed her eyes tightly as if to block out everything in her life. With her eyes closed, she did not see the car pull up and park. She did not see the four boys get out of the car and walk toward her. As her swing came slowly to a stop, she opened her eyes and jumped when she saw the boys.

"Hi, what's your name?" one of the boys asked. The taller boy said, "Don't be afraid, we came to Manfred to play and to make people feel better. Besides, you look like you could use a friend." The taller boy put out his hand and said, "Here we'd like you to try some of this and even give it to your friends. Just don't tell any adults, cuz they don't understand us kids."

The shorter boy went on to say, "We'll be back someday to see if you want any more of our 'feel good' candy." The taller boy laughed while he handed it to her. "Yeah, we'll come back each week to bring more. Next time you need to bring money, as much as you can get. The more money you have, the more candy you can buy."

As Val observed what was happening, she could not help crying out, "Teg, Esty — I have to go, I have to go down there. Tempest is in trouble!"

"No, it's not quite time. We need to wait a little longer. Remember, things happen for a reason," explained Esty.

The boys turned and walked back to their car and drove away. Tempest walked down to the river and sat on its bank. Crying, she took some of the drugs, put them in her mouth and swallowed them. The sun had set and it quickly got dark. She lay on her back to watch the clouds. Funny thing — she swore that she saw Val's face right before she fell asleep.

Meanwhile back at the Matador residence, Esther had awakened. "I feel fine, a little tired, but I'm okay,"

Marion was firm in her response. "Well, Mrs. Matador, I think we should see Dr. Lee first thing in the morning. You look as pale as a ghost does. As long as you feel okay, I'm off to bed. I'll see you in the morning."

As Marion left the room, Esther asked her husband, "Why do you have to be so hard on the children? I think that it's starting to affect them."

He seemed to be ignoring her. Not letting it bother her, she continued, "What is it going to take for you to understand? You just need to love Tempest. She looks to you and all you do is growl at her about everything she does."

Craig let out a heavy sigh. "She always seems to be lying and I've gotten tired of her stories. You rest. I'm going downstairs to wait for her to come home. I'll get her ready for bed."

The sun was down and the moon started to appear through the clouds as Craig paced the foyer waiting for Tempest to return.

"Blasted child — it's been hours since she ran out of here. She knows that she's supposed to be home by dark." Making himself even angrier he said, "I'll give you something to cry about, making your mother and me worry like this." He walked into the house; left the door unlocked, and shut off the porch light.

The house was quiet and Esther had fallen asleep. Marion had put Matt to bed, and she was sitting at the kitchen table. "You don't need to wait up, Marion. I'll see to it that Tempest gets to bed. Besides I have a few words for that girl."

"All right Mr. Matador. Good night," she replied. The grandfather clock chimed 11 o'clock and Craig started to pick up the phone and then slammed it down. He marched up the stairs and went to bed. "Blasted girl can sleep outside in the dark for all I care."

Val appeared by Tempest's side and picked up her hand. "Tempest I'm here and I'm not leaving until you wake up or someone finds you. It's not a cold night, so we'll be just fine."

M. FAYE WATERS

Chapter 17
Now What?

The next morning, Marion had already called her sister Nicci to come by the house to watch the kids while she went with Esther to the doctor. She thought to herself, "Mr. Matador is such a stubborn fool. He cannot possibly go into the clinic with us. Instead he'll drive us to the hospital and then go have coffee with the local men." The doorbell rang and Marion opened the door for her sister.

"Thanks for coming on such short notice," she said. "I'm going to go with Mrs. Matador to be with her. Just let the little darlings sleep late. Mr. Matador decided that they should stay home from school today. We'll call to let you know how long we will be."

Craig Matador dropped off his wife and Marion at the front door of the hospital. "I'll be back in an hour or so."

Two hours later, he drove through the drop off area looking for his wife and Marion. "Blasted, they must not be done." As he looked toward the entrance, Marion came out and waved to him.

She walked over to the car. "You'd better park the car, Mr. Matador. It's Mrs. Matador, she's not doing so well." Craig parked the car and walked with Marion into the clinic with neither uttering a word. He walked directly to Dr. Lee's office.

"Mr. Matador, come in and sit down," said Dr. Lee. "I'm afraid I have some good news and some bad news." Craig Matador looked him straight in the eye, and in a meeker voice than Marion ever remembered hearing from him said, "Well, you better give me the bad news first Doc."

"Your wife has a cyst that is putting pressure on her ovaries; and in most situations, we would operate to remove it right away. However, given her condition, it wouldn't be wise."

Craig interrupted. "Do it right away. Doc, you've got to do it right away."

Dr. Lee continued, "We would ... however, this is the good news. Your wife is expecting another baby."

Craig was shocked. "A baby, oh my God. Well what do we have to do?"

Dr. Lee replied, "I've called in a specialist and he will be here at 1 o'clock to see her. We'll run some more tests and then we will know our next steps. In the meantime we are going to admit her to the hospital so we can monitor her and the baby."

Chapter 18
Another Missing Person?

Nicci was playing cards with Matt when she asked, "Matt, does Tempest usually sleep this late?"

"Sometimes, but usually she's up earlier bugging me."

"It's almost 10:30 and we still haven't heard a peep from her. I had better go check."

As Nicci walked out of the room, Matt said desperately, "I wish we didn't have to wake her. It has been so nice and quiet without her. Sometimes, I wish I was the only kid in the family."

Nicci flashed him a reassuring smile. "Well, your life would be much more boring if that was the case. She's just trying to prove that she's the big sister."

Trying not to awaken her, Nicci opened the door quietly and slowly. As she peered into the room, she saw that Tempest's bed was perfectly straightened and Tempest was nowhere to be found. Nicci ran to see if the window was locked. It was. "What in the world is going on here?" she said to herself. The phone started ringing, so

Nicci left the room to answer it saying, "Matador Residence."

It was Marion. "Nicci, Mrs. Matador could really be sick."

As if she had not heard Marion at all, Nicci blurted out, "Tempest is gone, and she never slept in her bed last night."

"Oh my dear God!" cried out Marion, "Can you stay with Matt until I call back?"

"Yes, of course." Before she could say anything else, Marion had hung up the phone and was already running down the hall. She started pounding on Dr. Lee's door. Without waiting for a reply, she burst into the office and cried, "She's gone, Mr. Matador, she's gone. Tempest is gone." She walked right over and stood in front of Craig, "She didn't come home last night did she?"

Without answering her, Craig stood up and pushed by her as he ran out of the office.

He grabbed a phone book from the front counter and looked up Gene Sander's number. Gene was the owner of the other elevator, but he was also the only one who had bloodhounds. His dogs could track a person simply by smelling their scent from a piece of clothing. Craig Matador dialed Gene's number. "Say, Gene, this is Craig Matador. I need your help. My daughter didn't return from playing in the park last night. I was wondering if I could use your dogs to help find her." He shifted his body several times, as if he were crawling out of his skin. He was uncomfortable asking someone else for help. He also knew that he should never have gone to bed until Tempest was safe and sound in her bed.

"Well, I'm home giving my dogs a break. We're supposed to start looking for Val Flick again in a half hour."

Craig interrupted. "I don't care about Val." He stopped himself from saying more and continued, "Just let me have the dogs for one hour. I'll pay you $10,000."

Gene replied reluctantly, "Okay, I'll meet you by the park in ten minutes and we can look for both girls."

Craig ran out to the car thinking to himself, "In spite of being the wrong religion, maybe they're not such a bad family."

Gene was more than happy to help a neighbor, but he thought to himself as he hung up the phone, "Funny that he'd ask me for help. He sure didn't seem to like me or my dogs." Gene recalled the first night that the Matadors moved into the Nicholson mansion. The dogs were barking wildly at a raccoon that was in the garden. Craig came over, pounded on the door and told him to shut the dogs up or he would.

Gene left the house to get the dogs ready. "Oh well, forget about that night. This is Manfred and the people here are always willing to help out someone else who is in need."

He rounded up the dogs and headed for the park.

CHAPTER 19
LA LA LAND

Tempest slept very deeply as Val sat next to her, holding her hand. Tempest was dreaming that Val was trying to wake her up, but for some reason she could not bring herself to open her eyes. It was just like one of those dreams she had had where she was trying to get people to listen to her. No matter what she did or said, people ignored her. Even when she went to her dad's side and touched his arm, he acted as if she wasn't even there, shrugged her hand off and started talking to someone else. Funny though, she could feel someone holding her hand and yes, she could hear dogs barking. They sounded like they were getting closer and closer.

"Over there!" yelled Gene as he pointed toward the river. "The dogs must have picked up her scent, she's gotta be over there." Gene was right. After sniffing one of Tempest's sweaters, his dogs led them right to her.

Craig ran over kneeled down next to his daughter. Realizing that she was unconscious, he scooped her up into his arms and carried her to the car. "I need to get her to the hospital right away. Can someone call ahead and let them know that we are on our way?" He turned to Gene as he was getting into the car and said humbly, "Thanks Gene, I guess I owe you one and I'll get the money I promised to you as soon as I can."

Gene turned down Craig's offer. "There's no one keeping score here, it's all part of living in Manfred. We help each other out when people are in need. Now go and take care of your daughter!"

Once they got to the hospital, Tempest was laid on a gurney and wheeled away by a nurse. Another nurse instructed Craig to wait in the waiting room. He plopped himself in a chair, exhausted from the morning. "My God, what is going to happen next? My wife, my daughter and my baby are in danger. Dear God, please show me what has happened to my daughter. She is young and innocent. She needs to be home with her family – not in a hospital bed." His eyes filled with tears. "She belongs with the family who loves her." He bowed his head in his hands and closed his eyes.

"Mr. Matador, we need to get some information about your daughter, can you please come with me?" He looked up to see a young hospital employee standing over him. He followed her to an office, sat down and answered all of her questions. Once done he stood up and headed toward the door. "I need to go see my wife now."

Before he got halfway down the hall, he heard Dr. Lee's voice. "Mr. Matador, can you please step into my office?" Craig walked to Dr. Lee's office and leaned against the wall. "We had to pump your daughter's stomach. It appears that she attempted to overdose on some type of drug."

"Drug?" Craig yelled out.

"Yes, we sent her stomach contents to the lab to identify them. She is still sleeping, but she should be awake soon."

"Can I see her?"

The doctor nodded yes. "She's in room 107. Before you leave, Mr. Matador, you need to know that it is hospital policy to call the police if the drugs are a controlled substance. We will need to find out where she got them."

Craig walked out of the room with his shoulders drooped. As he got to room 107, his steps started to slow. He cautiously opened the door and walked to his daughter's bedside. As he bent his head, he started to cry. "Tempest, I have been so awful to you. I've been a bully, pigheaded and stubborn. I don't know why. Oh, oh I guess I do. You see my dad raised me this way, and it's all that I knew how to do. And I thought it was the way I needed to be in business to get things done." He took out a handkerchief and blew his nose. "All I know now is that I could lose you, your mom and our baby." He dropped in the chair beside her and held her hand as he continued. "I couldn't live without any of you. You are all that really matters to me in life. God knows that I would even give up the business to have you all healthy again. I swear, if we get out of this mess, I'm going to try to be a better person."

He laid his head back, exhausted, and fell asleep.

M. FAYE WATERS

Chapter 20
Out of the Dark

Val appeared in the hospital room and whispered quietly, "Tempest, you're going to be fine. You need to wake up now."

Craig, snoring lightly, was still dozing in the chair.

Val continued. "Your dad is here and he loves you very much. I think this time you can get him to change. Besides, your mom really needs to see you. Please Tempest, wake up!"

Tempest moaned and opened her eyes. "Ooohhh my stomach hurts."

She looked up and saw Val standing over her bed. "Well it's no wonder your stomach hurts. You should have seen what they had to do. They pumped out your stomach –and was that ever disgusting. Do not ever do that again, you had everyone worried. Do you know that you could have died? Promise me that you will never take drugs again! Oh, and for another thing, you're going to have to tell the police who gave you the drugs."

"But I don't know their names or where they live, or anything about them."

Val stood with her hands on her hips. "Now that's plain stupid, you're smarter than that. You never take anything from strangers even if it looks harmless or good to eat. Now think! What do you remember?"

Tempest squinted at Val, thinking hard. "I remember their car. It was loud when it drove away, so I looked up at it. It was black, had two doors and it had a dent in the back end. The license plate was from our state and had the number 3 and I think a G. Oh, and one of the mirrors looked broken."

"Which side?" asked Val.

Squinting hard, Tempest tried to remember, "It was on the driver's side."

"Now, that wasn't so hard, was it?" Val snorted. "Just remember that when the police talk to you."

Craig started to stir. Val quickly said, "Oops, I gotta go for now, but I'll be back." She leaned over and gave Tempest a hug.

When Val disappeared, Tempest leaned over and whispered in her dad's ear. "Daddy, Daddy. Wake up, Daddy."

Craig shook off the sleep and jumped to her bedside. "My little peach, I'm so glad that you're awake. What can I give you? Do you want a new doll, another game, a new bike, a pony? No, I know! We'll all go on a trip to Disney Land."

"No, Daddy. I do not want toys or trips. I just want you to stop being so cruel to people. I want you to do what you said you would do when I was sleeping. I want you to use integrity. I also want us to sell lentil seeds, and not ruin other people's farms and businesses."

Resorting back to his old ways, he started to object. "Tempest, you don't understand." Hesitating, he continued slowly, "Maybe you do understand. We can do all of that. It's just going to be different; but then, I promised you that I would change." He stopped and asked, "Say, when did you learn about integrity?"

Tempest chuckled. "You wouldn't believe me if I told you."

"I want to. I really want to," he said. "But it is difficult when you've made up so many stories that your mother and I can't tell the difference between what is real and not real. We never know when you're being honest with us."

Tempest looked sad. "I know, Dad, but I'm going to change that. I promise that I will be open and honest with you. I want you to trust me and what I say."

"Well we both have some changing to do. It is not always going to be easy, so we will need to rely on each other to let each other know if we are not keeping our word. I promise that I'll be patient with you and I'll take the time to really listen to you." Remembering his wife, he turned very solemn. "Right now I have something else important to talk to you about. It's about your mother."

Chapter 21
Almost Time to Go Home

Val, perched on top of a cloud with her arms crossed on her knees, sat holding her face in her hands looking sadly toward the ground.

Esty broke the silence. "I'm proud of you, Val. You really made a difference. I think Tempest and her Dad are really going to change."

Val perked up. "Do you really think so?"

"Yes, Val," added Teg. "He realizes how important integrity is. How human life and his family are more important than money. Tempest learned that she needs to be honest with people and to not make up stories or steal other people's property."

"Well there was one thing she did that I'm not so sure she has learned how to stop."

"What is that, Val?" asked Esty.

Val took a deep breath and remembered the painful experience of Tempest teasing Sally. "Tempest was teasing one of my best friends and I didn't do anything to stop her. Why is it that kids tease and hurt other kids?"

"I'm glad that you asked … it's something that children should learn about earlier in life rather than later." Esty went on to explain, "People make themselves feel better by putting others down. Unfortunately, they do not seem to understand that the feeling only lasts for a short time – and they do not realize how bad it makes them look. Some people misbehave just to get attention and some people act that way so they feel they are the ones in control."

"Wow that makes sense. Thanks for telling me!"

"It may take some time before Tempest and her father stop treating people as if they are inferior to them. It will take a conscious effort for them to choose to treat everyone kindly.

Meanwhile, Teg started sniffling and Esty joined him by casting Val a sad, yet reassuring look. They knew it was soon time for Val to go home. Esty took a long, deep breath and said, "It's almost time for you to go home. We are going to miss you, but we want you to know that we will be watching over you every day. Sometimes we will even wave to you… just as we did before. Val, we are all connected to each other and nothing will ever change that. We are in your heart and in your soul, and you will always feel our presence.

"Are you sure that you'll never forget me?" Val asked.

Esty quickly replied, "Never."

"Not in a million years?" Val asked. "Never?" After a slight pause, Val continued, "Knock-Knock."

"Who's there?" replied Esty.

"See, you forgot me already!" exclaimed Val. They all laughed joyfully.

"We're running out of time," said Teg. "Before you can see your family, you have several things to do. You know what you have to do now. You need to make things right with Betty and we need to talk more about Tempest."

Teg added, "You need to help Tempest and Craig Matador. People think that people can make a life by earning money. Money is certainly needed to buy the necessities in life, but life is more than that. People make a life by what they GIVE! You have truly given a great gift to Tempest and her family ... a gift that has changed their lives. They now know that it is not about the money. It's about living a life with honesty and living a life full of integrity."

"Val, it's all about saying the truth," added Esty. "It's about being sincere, upfront about the facts and not being deceitful."

"Integrity is not only doing what you say you are going to do, when you say you'll do it...it's about doing the right thing without others asking you to." Teg beamed down at Val as he added the final lesson. "Honor your self, honor your word."

They both hugged her while Esty said, "Now go ... it is time."

Chapter 22
Making it Right

Tempest finished dressing and threw her hospital gown on the bed just as there was a knock on her door. Before she could say anything, there was another knock at the door. Tempest asked, "Who's there?"

Marion replied from the other side, "Olive."

Tempest, knowing it was Marion, asked, "Olive, who?"

Marion, smiling and walking through the door answered, "Olive you!" Tempest ran toward Marion and hugged her saying, "I am so glad to see you."

Matt, who stood behind Marion not knowing what to think of this happy Tempest, kept his arms wrapped tightly around Marion. Seeing her little brother, Tempest moved toward him. He dropped his arms from Marion and backed away. "Wait, what are you going to do to me?"

"Don't be silly. I am done being mean and nasty to you. Honestly! I learned some new words – honesty and integrity.

Imagine that. I said honesty." Tempest chuckled to herself. "From now on I'm going to only say the truth. Dad is going to help me remember to be honest and I'm going to help him use integrity."

"Ooo-kay. But what do you mean by 'in teg ri tee'?" asked Matt.

"Its integrity, spelled I-N-T-E-G-R-I-T-Y and it means that he's going to do what he says he's going to do and he'll do it when he says he will. It means honoring your word."

Tempest turned to Marion. "I'm really sorry for the times that I've been mean or have lied to you."

"Dear child, I am so glad to hear that. I always knew you had a good soul. You just needed to let everyone else see it." Feeling compassion for the young girl, she knew it was soon time to take her and her brother to their mother.

At that moment, Craig entered the room. He walked over to his daughter, hugged her, and said, "Tempest I'm so happy that you are going to be okay. I love you very much and don't want anything bad to ever happen to you again. You need to know that you could have died. I hope that you learned to never take any type of pill from anyone other than those you know and trust." Turning to Matt he said, "Matt, do you also understand what happened and what not to do?"

Matt nodded his head. "Yes, I think I do."

"That's good," said Craig. "I couldn't bear it if anything happened to either of you. I really need to know that you got it. Matt, could you please tell me what you think the lesson is behind this?"

"Okay Dad. I know that I should never accept anything from strangers, especially something that looks like drugs or even candy.

And yes, I know that drugs can really hurt, if not kill, people.

Feeling that they really did understand, his thoughts went to his wife. He sighed heavily and said, "It's time that we talk about your mother. Let's sit down for a few minutes. Last night your mother fainted — so we brought her in to see Dr. Lee this morning. They are keeping her overnight as they continue running some tests. They found a lump in her body that they are testing. We should know more tomorrow." Sounding excited, he continued, "But I have some great news. Your mother is expecting another baby. So that means you're going to have a baby sister or brother."

"Yeah – that is going to be so much fun! I would love to have a baby sister or brother to help take care of. Can we go see Mom now? I can't wait to hug her and let her know that I'm going to be the best big sister ever," Tempest remarked.

Her father replied, "Not for a couple of hours. She is sleeping and Dr. Lee asked us to come back later. We are going to go home for a while. But on the way home, we need to stop at the General Store and pick up a few things."

Tempest could not wait for their car to stop in front of the store. She knew it was time to talk to Betty.

The family got out the car and walked into the store. Craig explained to Tempest, "Marion is going to the grocery section and Matt and I are going to the hardware area. You can come with us or meet us when we're done."

Tempest, knowing what she had to do, happily replied, "I'm going to talk to Betty."

Hearing her name, Betty looked up to see Tempest walking

toward her. Before Tempest had a chance to say anything Betty said, "How about some hot apple cider? I just happen to have some in this pot. Now you come over and get yourself a cup." Not knowing what to say, Tempest remained quiet as they sipped on their cider.

"Your father told me what is going on with your mother," Betty said softly. "I'm sure it's really scary not knowing if your mother is okay. I lost my mother to cancer when I was just a young girl. I remember how awful it felt and how all that I wanted was for her to be okay. Research has come very far and there are many new treatments. I'm sure she'll be fine."

"Yeah, it sounds like the doctor thinks she'll be okay. I am sorry to hear about your mom. I don't even want to think what it would be like without my mom."

Betty put her arm around Tempest. "I have a really strong feeling that your mom will be just fine."

"I think so. I can really feel it." Tempest paused while she worked up the courage to apologize. "Betty, there's something that I really need to talk to you about. Something that is really bugging me 'cause it wasn't right."

"What is it?"

Tempest looked down at her hands as she continued. "Remember that day when Val and I were in the store… it was the day that your ankle was sore and you told me to pick out the candy I wanted and to bring it to you?"

Betty nodded suspiciously. "Yes. Yes I do."

Tempest continued. "Well — I made Val put some candy in her pants because I told her that she owed me. I know she did not want to but I did not give her a choice. She felt terrible and she wanted me to tell you. She said that I needed to be honest with you and that she was also going to tell you when she gets home that she is sorry about what she did."

Tears welled up in Betty's eyes as she thought about Tempest's apology, but also about the fact that she missed Val terribly. She looked at Tempest and said, "Thank you for telling me the truth. It's so important to be honest and I'm so glad that you told me."

"Another thing, I took one of your Halloween decorations too. It was one of those glow-in-the-dark skeletons."

Craig called out to them, "Well, Betty, I think we've got what we need for now. Come on Tempest! Let's get ready to go home."

Before Tempest left, she looked at Betty sheepishly. "Thanks for being so nice about it. I swear that I'll do whatever you want me to do to make up for what we took."

"Let me think about it. I'm sure we can come up with something."

As the family left, Betty could not help but think, "What did she mean she talked to Val and that she was going to talk to me when she got home?"

She shook her head and thought she heard Val's voice say, "Hello Betty." She heard it again and turned around to see Val's smiling face. Val ran into her arms. "Oh Betty, I missed you so much."

Betty looked astonished, but hugged Val close. "Where on God's green earth have you been? We have all been so worried about you."

"It's hard to explain, but what's important is that I'm home," said Val. "I haven't even seen my mom and dad yet, but I heard you and Tempest talking and I wanted to tell you how sorry I am. I knew it was wrong and I will never take anything that is not mine ever again. Tempest and I will work off what we owe you by helping you out in the store. I am truly sorry — I really understand now how important it is to be honest, but I really need to go now. I can't wait to see my mom, dad and Reese."

"Okay Val. We can talk more at another time. It's important for you to go home and let your family know that you are okay. I'll see you soon!" Watching Val leave, Betty mumbled in her mind, "Such curious children. They both talked about the importance of honesty. Well, if that is the case, I hope it is in the water. We can all use a strong dose of honesty in this world."

Chapter 23
I'm Home

Val could hardly wait to get into the house. "Mom! Dad! Reese! Are you home?"

They all immediately came running out of the kitchen. Crying and screaming with happiness, her mother reached her first. She grabbed Val in a huge bear hug. "We were so afraid that something happened to you!"

Her father reached her next. "We looked everywhere for you. Where have you been? We are so happy you are home. I am sure glad we were home when you got here. We just stopped for a quick bite to eat."

"We spent every night camped out looking for you and hoping we'd find you," Reese added as they all continued to hug each other.

"Where have you been?" Al asked.

Jean interrupted, "That's not important right now. She is home and safe and I am sure she will explain everything to us. The lasagna will not be ready for another twenty minutes. Why don't we let her take a bath and get cleaned up? Then we can hear all about it.

Al reluctantly agreed, "Okay, I guess that can wait."

Jean turned back to Val somewhat baffled saying, "Although I must say you look pretty good for being gone a couple of days."

Before her mother could ask any questions, Val broke away from the hug. "That would be really nice, Mom. Dad, Reese, I'll be back." She turned and walked with her mother to the bathroom.

"I'm going to find Snowball for Val, as I'm sure she'll be happy to see her too." Reese offered as he went off to find the cat. Just then, the doorbell rang. Al turned to open the door and was surprised to see his father standing there. "Hello, Al, I'd like to talk with you and find out what I can do to help find Val." Handing him the plant he had purchased from Betty he added, "Here this is for you and your family."

Al motioned Ray inside. "Thanks. Come on in. You'll be happy to know that Val just got home. She went to take a bath and get cleaned up."

Ray grabbed his son and gave him a big hug. "That's great Son. I just knew she'd be okay." Sensing that Al was still upset with him he continued, "Now that she's home we need to talk."

"Yes — that would be a great idea. Let's go out in the back yard." The two men headed out the back door.

"I am really sorry that I wasn't here for you, Al. I did return home a couple of times, and when I saw you, I didn't know what to say. The best thing I can do is to be honest with you and tell you that it was never about you. It was about me finding out who I am and what I wanted out of life. It was very selfish of me and I deeply regret not being a part of your life. But I'm back and I want to make it up to you."

Al sat for a while staring at the swing and tree house. He finally said, "I remember when we made this swing and put it up. After you left, I would swing every night that I could. I am sure that I had swung for miles and miles, enough miles to find you, but I never did. I really missed you, Dad."

"I missed you, too!" replied Ray. He continued, "I know that an apology isn't enough, so I'm asking that you give me a chance. Let me share in your life and the lives of your family. Let me prove to you how much I care about all of you."

After a long pause, Al stood up. Finally, he said, "Well we do have a small trailer home that you could move into. I suppose we can try it for a while. I know that Val and Reese would really like to have their grandfather around — and I would like to have my father around." He reached out and gave his father a hug. "Welcome home, Dad!"

Chapter 24
The Future is Bright

Sheriff Hoekstra had just finished writing down everything that Tempest could remember about that awful night in the park. As he stood to leave, he solemnly stated, "Tempest, it's critical that we find the boys who gave you the drugs. You seem to remember a lot and with what you've told us, I'm confident we'll be able to find them quickly." He shook Craig's hand and also put out his hand to shake Tempest's hand saying, "I'll be sure to keep you and your family informed. Thanks again . . . and Tempest I hope you feel better soon. You do look like you could use some more rest."

"Thank you, Sheriff, and be sure to let us know if we can do anything else," stated Craig as he walked him to the door.

Tempest really was exhausted, but managed to say, "Good-bye, Sheriff Hoekstra. I can't wait to hear that you've found those guys."

As the Sheriff drove away, Tempest turned to Marion who had just walked into the foyer. "I'm kind of tired. I'm going to my room."

Marion walked over and hugged the girl. "Okay dear, you rest for a while. Everyone knows that you deserve it." She left to pick up the ringing phone. "Hello?... Yes, I will get her for you. Tempest you have a phone call."

Tempest answered the phone upstairs, "Hello?"

Val quickly blurted out, "Hello Tempest, I'm home now and I am supposed to be taking a bath. But I want to know how it went with your Dad after I left."

"Well it went pretty well. He and I agreed to help each other to be honest with everyone and to use integrity everyday! It's not going to be easy, but I'll do my best. We made a deal that if we slip, we'll remind each other of what just happened."

"That sounds like a great deal!" exclaimed Val. "I better get back to my bath. See you later."

"That Val is definitely going to be my BFF. I've never really had one before," muttered Tempest as she crawled into the comfort of her bed.

Val quickly finished her bath and went downstairs to join her family. Reese and Jean were the first to sit down for the evening meal. Val joined them asking, "Where's dad?"

Al walked in with his father saying, "I have some great news to share. Kids, this is your grandfather, Ray. He has been away for many years, but now he's home." With admiration Al continued, "Dad, this is my wife, Jean. Our son, Reese and of course, you've heard about our daughter, Val – since you helped to look for her."

As they stood up to greet Ray, he walked to each of them and gave them a hug saying, "I am so happy to be here and I have no intentions of ever leaving again." He flashed Al a reassuring smile.

"Welcome to our home and to our family!" Jean said as she hugged him.

In unison, Val and Reese exclaimed, "Welcome!" They were both excited that their grandfather had chosen to return to Manfred to live.

"Let's eat before this great looking meal gets cold," Al said as he motioned for everyone to sit down. "We've got a lot of catching up to do."

He folded his hands and bowed his head saying, "God, thank you for returning Val to us and for helping my father find his way home. We are truly grateful for this food and all of your blessings. Amen."

The family anxiously waited for Val to tell them everything that had happened to her and where she was. However, they also wanted to hear more about Ray, their grandfather.

Reese could not wait another minute, "Okay Val. You have to tell us where you were. We looked everywhere for you. We even went to Mrs. Palmer's house. In unison, they agreed that they wanted to hear her story.

"Can we eat dessert first?" Val asked.

Jean stood up asking, "Who's ready for some angle food cake with fresh strawberries?"

"That sounds absolutely wonderful! My favorite food is dessert," stated Ray.

Everyone had finished dessert and Val took that as a cue to share her story. She started out very cautiously, "Okay – it's time I tell you what happened. You know how you always tell me the importance of telling the truth and how telling the truth and being honest doesn't hurt?" She paused then continued, "Well, I'm just afraid you won't believe me."

"Val, please tell us and we'll believe you." Al assured her.

"Okay. It is going to take some explaining, cuz at times – I felt that I was in a dream. But it really did happen." After pausing again she continued, "Here it is. I have two new friends who found me and took great care of me. They taught me two very important lessons. One was about honesty and the other was about integrity. I kept meeting up with Tempest to help her and her father learn how to live their lives by being honest and practicing integrity. By the way, I did see that the three of you were okay and I am sorry that I worried you. I wanted to come home . . . but we were on a mission to help the Matador family. Mr. Matador and Tempest both are trying to be better people. Once you see them, you'll understand."

Jean exclaimed, "Tell us who these wonderful people are and where they live so we can properly thank them."

Val reminded them, "You said you would believe me – right?"

Al answered firmly, "Right!"

"My new friends live in the clouds," Val proclaimed.

The trio sat there stunned. Reese was the first to reply, "We believe you Val. After all, you have watched and talked to the clouds for years."

Jean added, "It is true. Ever since you were a baby, you loved to sit and watch the sky. It seemed to fascinate you for hours.

"Well, I guess that it explains it!" Al confirmed. "We are just happy that you are safe and home with us." Still mystified like the other two, he chose to let it be.

"I'm really tired and can't wait to go to bed. Would it be okay to miss school tomorrow?" Val continued, "Besides I'm not ready to tell everyone where I was at. It should be our secret for now. Cuz some people might not understand and they'll think I'm crazy."

Jean reassured her, "I think everyone will understand that you need to rest. I'll call Mrs. Rogness in the morning."

"It's time that we all go to bed and get some rest," Al added.

The family hugged each other good night as they each went to their respective rooms feeling grateful for Val's safe return.

Chapter 25
A Great Day for a Celebration

The next morning, there was a knock at Tempest's bedroom door. Her father walked in and sat on her bed. "Good morning sleepy head. We checked on you a couple of times but you were sound asleep so we just let you sleep and miss school today. I have great news for you. I just talked with Dr. Lee and your mother is going to be fine. In fact, I'm going to go pick her up and bring her home while you eat some breakfast." He glanced at his watch. "Or maybe I should say brunch."

"Oh, Dad, that is great news about Mom. Are you sure that I can't come with you to pick her up?"

"You stay here and help Marion. Everyone is getting together this evening in the park to celebrate that you and Val are home safe and sound."

Tempest gave her dad a morning hug saying, "That sounds like a great time! It will be nice to see Val again."

"Yes it will be fun. Especially now . . . that your mother is going to be fine. I need to leave for the hospital, so I'll see you when we get home."

The community was bustling with activity, as everyone was getting ready to celebrate the safe return of both girls.

Ray had a few items to pick up at the General Store, and was in no hurry to pay for them. He tipped his hat as he approached the cash register. "Good afternoon, Betty. I came by to get a few things and to see what I can do to help you out."

"You're just in time," she replied. "I really could use your help getting ready for the picnic. My Uncle Roger and his kids are on their way to keep the store open. You can help me bring out the rest of the things."

Ray smiled as he followed Betty to the back of the store.

Soon crowds of people began to gather and the picnic started. After everyone had gotten their food and was sitting down to eat, Mayor Beilke, Sheriff Hoekstra, Craig Matador and Al Flick stood on the stage to address the crowd.

Mayor Beilke spoke first. "Thank you everyone for coming out today to celebrate the safe return of Val and Tempest. Let us allow them to enjoy the evening and not ask them many questions. Both Al and Craig have something to share with you and then we will hear from Sheriff Hoekstra. So let's get started."

Al took the microphone next. He looked gratefully at the crowd and stated, "We really appreciated everyone helping us to look for our daughters. We never gave up hope and regardless of where they were or what happened, the important thing is ...that Val and

Tempest are both safe and at home with their families."

Shifting his weight, he paused and sounding choked up, he added, "It was such an inspiration to see how this community joined together. You should all be commended." Recovering from the emotion of the moment, he concluded, "Thank you."

Craig then took the microphone from Al. "Well, Al, at least you've been a great father. I let Tempest down by not talking to her about this issue of drugs. Believe me – now Matt and Tempest both understand the dangers of drugs. To all of you kids out there, please listen to your parents and listen to me when I tell you...leave as soon as you see that there are drugs in the area. Get away and call the police or your parents. Whatever you do, don't take anything, even if it looks like candy, and certainly don't take pills from anyone other than your parents or a doctor."

Sheriff Hoekstra asked if he could address the crowd. Craig handed him the microphone.

"Since we're on the topic of drugs...we are happy to inform you that we have arrested the kids who came to Manfred and gave Tempest the drugs. Tempest, you are quite the brave girl by telling us all you remembered. Based on the information you gave us, we notified the Drug Enforcement Agency or, as we refer to it, the DEA. They had been suspicious of and were watching a group of kids from Brownstown, but they never had any hard evidence. They set up a trap, also known as a sting operation in Gooseberry Park. The kids fell for it, and not only were they arrested, but they gave the detectives the names of their suppliers. We will not even need to involve you or your family. Kids — once again please do not become involved with drugs. As Craig stated, if you see or hear about them, talk with your parents or the police."

Craig was not done yet. He took back the microphone. "I have something else I'd like to share. After nearly losing Tempest and with my wife getting ill . . . then getting better, I have learned some valuable lessons. Being honest and maintaining integrity every day with my family…and all of you…is more important than making a huge profit in business. I would like to announce that my brother and I will only start businesses that will complement the others in town. We will be offering lentil seeds and will be hosting several seminars on how to enhance your farming operations with them.

"Okay, I need to stop, as I'm starting to sound like a commercial. I just have a few more things to say. I'm asking for your forgiveness for being rude and a bully. I want you to know that I am committed to being a better person. I realize that it is not just my words that are important … but it is my actions too. I have a big ego, so this is a big change for me, and I will need your support. Feel free to let me know when I falter. Thanks again, Gene … we would not have found Tempest if it was not for you and your dogs. I will always remember your compassion – and just know that I will offer my help to any of you – whenever you need it."

Al put his arm around Craig's shoulder. "Now that's an offer if I've ever heard one." He chuckled and continued, "We have all learned some great lessons over the past few days. Respecting and cherishing your family and friends is the first one, so with that, I think it is time that we enjoy spending time with each other. In fact, Val tells us that once we have time together as a family, she has a lot more to share with us about her little adventure…and I for one…can't wait to hear more." To move the celebration along, he proclaimed,

"It's time for this celebration to end with a big bang. Luckily it gets dark early, so we'll have some fireworks, courtesy of Matador Enterprises, and then we'll get our kids home and off to bed early for school in the morning. Good night everybody and thanks again!"

The sun had slipped behind the horizon leaving a beautiful orange glow illuminating the clouds with streaks of light and color. As Val wandered away from the crowd to watch the colors fade, she thought of her puffy cloud friends and all that she had learned from her adventures with them. She could not help wishing that she would be swooshed up into the clouds to visit them once again. She felt a great sense of accomplishment as she truly did add value to someone else's life. In fact, she helped an entire family. The rush of pride inside of her made her want to continue on the journey of making a positive difference in the world. She knew that she had not seen the last of Esty and Teg. She also knew that she was not done and that there is a lot more to do. She sighed impatiently, "I can hardly wait to find out what is next."

The sky continued to darken and the crowd was ready for the evening finale. As Val made her way back to her family, the sky began to erupt with beautiful flashing fireworks. Streaks of red, blue, green and gold cut across the sky. A large gold, tree-like glow erupted, a second and then a third time, as the crowd cheered. Everyone stood mesmerized by the display of Old Glory, many of them reflecting on how grateful they were to have the life they do and for the experience they had collectively gone through. Having gone through the experience, the community had grown closer than ever. The story of Val and Tempest would certainly be talked about for a very long time.

Val and her family sat on a blanket with their arms wrapped around each other for comfort and warmth – all of them enjoying the show.

Jean commented quietly, "This is so beautiful. It's great to imagine how wonderful of a life we have in Manfred."

"Yeah Mom – jiiT-Now! Which means – 'just imagine it now.' " Val confidently added.

Val glanced at the dark sky opposite the fireworks display. What was that? She looked again and could have sworn she saw a wave and a wink from the only two clouds left in the sky.

Jean replied, "I love it. What a great new word that means so much! jiiT-Now."

JUST IMAGINE

POINTS TO PONDER

HERE ARE SOME GREAT TOPICS FOR YOU TO DISCUSS WITH EACH OTHER:

- It's good for you to take time each day to just be still and to take in the sights and sounds around you. (Page 2)

- It's all a part of helping out in this family. (Page 5)

- By simply being grateful and acknowledging what we have, we will attract true wealth and abundance. (Page 11)

- I really wish that people didn't make judgments about others without knowing all the facts. (Page 18)

- Haven't you ever heard of 'guilty by association'? (Page 22)

- We need to learn from our mistakes. (Page 26)

- It must be difficult for her to look into a mirror and be happy with her life and herself. (Page 27)

- Wouldn't it be great if everyone respected each other and each other's property? (Page 28)

- I would rather that you guess and be wrong than not participate in the classroom. (Page 35)

- Hate: Those are some pretty strong words. (Page 36)

- Integrity means that you actually do what you say you are going to do when you say you will. (Page 46)

- Everyone needs to be responsible for what they say and do. (Page 55)

- Just don't tell any adults, cuz they don't understand us kids. (Page 82)

- People make themselves feel better by putting others down. (Page 100)

- People make a life by what they give. (Page 101)

- We have all learned some great lessons over the past few days. Respecting and cherishing your family and friends is the first one. (Page 122)

- Think of the traditions or rituals that you share in your family. What other traditions can you create together?

- Talk about not using drugs and alcohol – instead finding other ways to feel "high" about life – perhaps through creative arts, through sports, or through practicing "The Gift of Love" as described on another page in this book.

M. FAYE WATERS

JUST IMAGINE

About the cover artwork:

Hans Gilsdorf, a.k.a. Gilly, is an artist that has created art for movies, zoos, museums, churches, hospitals and private collectors. But after his first daughter was born five weeks premature, Hans became more focused on creating art to help children undergoing medical treatment.

"I really wanted to find a way to use my talents to make a difference for kids," Hans realized. The result is Gilly Art. Hans' vision of using art as a distraction tool for children by integrating it in the medical environment creates a kid-friendly, family-centered atmosphere that fosters healing. With Gilly Art installations in hospitals like Fargo's MeritCare Children's Hospital and St. Mary's Innovis Health in Minnesota, the smiles on the children's faces are proof that Gilly Art does make a difference.

Recently, Hans has collaborated with others who have a passion for helping kids by bringing life to their work through his art and character design.

Hans works from his lake home/studio in Detroit Lakes, Minnesota - enjoying small town life with his wife, Mary Beth, and their two daughters, Kendra and Megan.

To learn more about Hans, visit his website at www.hansgilsdorf.com.

M. FAYE WATERS

Welcome to The Gift of Love Project!

We invite you to read and practice the process described in The Gift of Love as you find it on the next page.

We ask you to read aloud "The Gift of Love" daily for 30 days WITH YOUR FAMILY. Just like when reading "*Just Imagine: Adventures with Teg and Esty*", sometimes parents read to children; if prepared to do so, sometimes children read to parents.

Take a moment daily after reading it and look into each others' eyes and feel the goodness, feel the love. Only GOOD can come from this powerful yet sweet family practice.

If you are interested in further information, simply go to www.FayeWaters.com and click on the link for www.TheGiftofLove.com.

JUST IMAGINE

THE GIFT OF LOVE

I Agree Today To Be The Gift of Love.

I Agree to Feel Deeply Love for Others Independent of Anything They are Expressing, Saying, Doing, or Being.

I Agree to Allow Love As I Know It To Embrace My Whole Body And Then to Just Send It To Them Silently and Secretly.

I Agree to Feel It, Accept It, Breathe It Into Every Cell of My Body on Each In-Breath And On Each Out-Breath Exhale Any Feeling Unlike Love.

I Will Repeat This Breathing Process Multiple Times Until I Feel it Fully and Completely Then Consciously Amplify in Me The Feeling of Love and Project It to Others As The Gift of Love.

This is My Secret Agreement – No One Else Is To Know it.

May be reproduced in totality for any peaceful purpose without financial gain. All rights reserved, Jerome DeShazo, D.D., M.B.A.,M.C.C.

Do You Need a Speaker?

Do you want M. Faye Waters to speak to your group or event? Then contact Larry Davis at: **(623) 337-8710** or email: **ldavis@intermediapr.com** or use the contact form at: **www.intermediapr.com**.

Whether you want to purchase bulk copies of *Just Imagine* or buy another book for a friend, get it now at: **www.imprbooks.com**.

If you have a book that you would like to publish, contact Terry Whalin, Publisher, at Intermedia Publishing Group, (623) 337-8710 or email: twhalin@intermediapub.com or use the contact form at: www.intermediapub.com.

M. Faye Waters
水

Just Imagine is more than just a book – it is an opportunity to connect with your family more deeply – to open communication on some of today's tough topics that often get skipped over. *Just Imagine* opens the door for reading together, talking together, and being together for even twenty minutes each day, sharing something precious – your presence, appreciation and love.

M. Faye Waters is taking a stand to awaken humanity's sense of pride, family and community – pride that we, as adults, are exemplifying honorable character and values for our youth.

Just Imagine could be acted out at a slumber party skit with different kids reading parts or it could be turned into a school play. You can take turns reading it out loud to each other. Use the *Points to Ponder* to embrace and evolve the connection you have with your children. Use it as a study guide in your place of fellowship.

Notice the Chinese/Japanese writing of the word "water" – the symbol for water in the logo. Our planet and our bodies are predominantly water. Water is used richly in every spiritual tradition. Water is commonly associated with the human qualities of intuition and imagination. Every country, every culture and every person needs water to survive and to thrive, just as we need quality of character. The story of *Just Imagine* can take place anyplace in the world just as the issues of dishonesty, lack of integrity and substance abuse occur anywhere in the world. Let us all use our wisdom to enhance the connections between cultures as we go through this journey called life. And together let's answer the higher calling that inspires us to transform ourselves, our children and our world.